THE CASCADES

A Natural Heritage

To Kristen,

Enjoy The Cascades!

K. Scott Ziegler

K. SCOTT ZIEGLER

To my parents,
who opened the door for me to visit
these places of beauty and mystery.

This book would not have been possible without the help of Kathy Springmeyer, with the assistance of Shirley Machonis and Jessica Solberg of Farcountry Press. Thanks to Kurt Sontag for reviewing the manuscript.

Maps were made from 1:250,000 Scale Digital Elevation Models available from the U.S. Geological Society.
Photographs were made from 4x5 and 8x10 size color transparencies, 1979—2003.
Front cover: *William O. Douglas Country: Subalpine firs, Dewey Lake, Ridges of the Naches drainage*
Back cover: *(left) Mt. Baker from above Swift Creek*
　　　　(right) Heather and huckleberry, Illswoot Lake, Skykomish Watershed

ISBN: 1-59152-009-6
© 2004 by K. Scott Ziegler
All rights reserved.

Created, produced, and designed in the United States.
Distributed by Farcountry Press, Helena, MT 59601 (800) 821-3874
Printed in China.

Avalanche lilies at Mirror Lake, Mt. Rainier National Park

4 *Mountain hemlocks and Pacific silver firs on Johnson Ridge, Skykomish watershed*

Table of Contents

SECTION I divides the Washington Cascades into the most prominant watersheds—those areas of land that drain into the major river systems that either flow into the Columbia River or into Puget Sound.

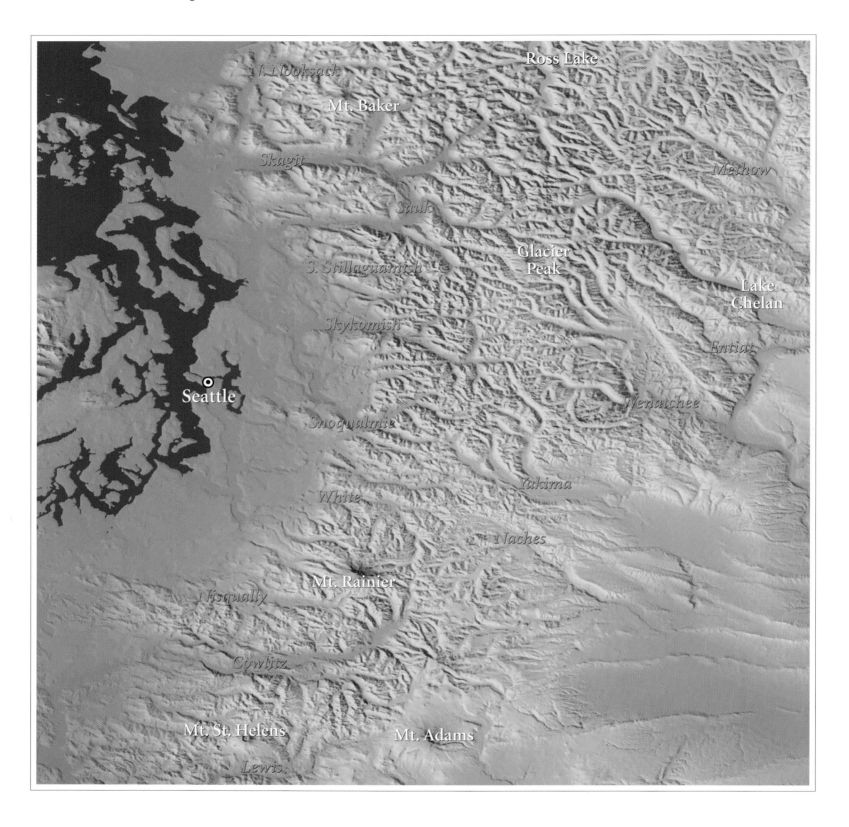

Map of the Washington Cascades Watersheds

Mt. Shuksan from the North Fork of the Nooksack Valley

Nooksack

ONE OF THE MAGNIFICENT RIVER SYSTEMS springing from the glacier-gouged highlands, the Nooksack drains a formidable section of the North Cascades. Its headwaters are set at the base of two mountains of dramatic, natural presence: Mt. Shuksan and Mt. Baker. The land it occupies is usually soaking wet, if not buried under snow, and commonly supports the exuberant growth of western hemlocks, Douglas firs, Pacific silver firs, western red cedars, and mountain hemlocks— evergreen trees that flourish and are entirely at home in the ever-pervading dankness. Moist flows of air, which originate in the Pacific directly to the west and to the southwest, condense profuse amounts of precipitation as they climb the westerly slopes. Winter storms dump prodigious amounts of snow that accumulate at higher elevations to a common mid-winter depth of twenty feet or more.

Shuksan and Baker are often hidden by high hills at close range, but they loom large over the deeply cut North Fork. Of all the major peaks in the Cascades, Shuksan is the only one that still holds its original Indian name, commonly translated as "Roaring Mountain." One of the highest non-volcanic peaks in the Cascades, this ice-sculpted peak of metamorphosed basalt reveals magnificent aspects through the shifting seasons of sun and snowstorms. The blank, dark pinnacle of the Nooksack Tower, part of a dangerous-looking north wall, rises above a stark, lonesome cirque of rock and ice and battered brush that is the source of the North Fork.

As in other areas of the North Cascades, initial explorations of the Nooksack concerned finding an overland route and searching for precious metals. But not all explorers were motivated by economic interests in the nineteenth century. Edmund Coleman attempted to climb Mt. Baker three times, which is to say he set off on three different expeditions to the unexplored territory of the Cascades. His expeditions involved traveling by boat from his hometown of Victoria across Puget Sound to a jumping off place at the town of Whatcom (Bellington). It then involved a combination of canoeing the waterways and fighting through the mostly pathless vegetation until reaching the subalpine meadows and glaciers. He made his first attempt up the Skagit River, the second up the North Fork of the Nooksack, and the last and successful attempt in 1868 up the Middle Fork of the Nooksack.

Coleman possessed an artist's ability to observe and translate his experience, as shown from his sketches and writings. His expressions reflect the European romantic view of nature of his times: that the individual can do significant things, and that mountains can be "conquered." To his imagination the unexplored wildlands of the Cascades were full of hostility, a domain of powerful forces, a wild, desolate realm of weather and volcanism where human beings ventured at considerable risk. Indeed, at the time of Coleman's explorations, the interior of the range was still the Great Unknown.

> *"Here we leave the outskirts of civilization; our path henceforward will be through a howling wilderness tenanted by wild animals, through dense and trackless forests where the light of sun never enters, across maddening torrents and precipitous rapids, and along overhanging precipices. We have to deal with nature in her sternest aspects - torn and convulsed, at war with herself, bearing on her face the scars of countless ages of desolating power, of the flood of the avalanche, and the burning tempest."*

The description may seem somewhat ludicrous to us today, but Coleman had fewer established certainties on which to rely. The natives, whom the explorers relied upon for direction, did not venture beyond certain heights, convinced that the mountaintops were the sole domain of a spirit that defied trespass. But for Coleman, as with other explorers new to the Northwest, the wild Cascades represented a place where he could test his mettle, survive uncertainty, use his judgment to circumvent dangers, and return in tact to the comforts of civilization. He had moved to Victoria with the expressed intention of scaling the glaciated peaks of the Cascades in the same way as he had ascended the Alps. By the time of his arrival, he had already overcome many of the fears and superstitions stirred by mountains (such as Mt. Blanc) certainly no less intimidating in appearance than Mt. Baker.

Unlike today's popular approach routes, which provide a thoroughfare through the jungles, no smooth highways or even approach trails were available at the time of Coleman's expeditions. After fighting against the currents and rapids of the Middle Fork of the Nooksack as far as his group could, they had to contend with the undergrowth of the deep valleys, always dense (lucky for them not soaking wet), with many downed logs rotting and covered with moss. In the Nooksack River valleys, streambanks are, as a rule, jungly and impenetrable, and there are swampy bogs rife with the barbs of devil's club. As far away in distance and in effort as they were from any settlement, Coleman was amazed to see his Indian guides grow indignant at tree blazes, evidence to them that another tribe was invading their hunting territory.

They left the shelter of the Middle Fork Valley and started up the steep slope beneath the umbrage of Douglas firs, silver firs, and then mountain hemlocks on a dismal mountain day when it chilled them to stop and rest. Coleman added drama and exaggeration by quoting words of Thomas Carlyle: "Yes, to me also was given, if not Victory, yet the consciousness of Battle, and the resolve to persevere therein. . . ." Having broken out of the trees where their view was mostly obscured by fog, he exclaimed: "Many valleys have I seen, but this was the best illustration of 'Beauty sleeping in the lap of Terror.'" His party had by this time reached the lush flower meadows growing in the wake of the glistening, crevassed glaciers below the jagged dark rock of the Black Buttes, the ice extending far beyond where it ends today.

Considering his past attempts to reach the summit of Mt. Baker, fear and exaggeration of dangers seem somewhat justifiable. On the second attempt, he spent a frightfully cold night on the icy saddle that now bears his name, jumping up and down to stay alive in the below-freezing air. Also, it had been about twelve years since his youthful exploits in the Alps, and along with age (he was into his forties by this time), sedentary town life had worn on him. The group used his equipment—ice axe, creepers (an early form of crampons), and rope—to wind their way through the crevasses on the hard snow. It was a wild place by any account. Were the tracks that his companion Thomas Stratton followed truly grizzly bear tracks? On one of his other trips, he had plainly seen tracks of an elk and wolf leading to blood-stained snow where a scuffle had ensued. Did a large eagle actually swoop down over Stratton while he was waiting for his companions?

Stratton provided the impetus they needed to push over the final obstacle, painstakingly cutting steps for two hours. For a few breathtaking moments they all watched helplessly as a huge block of ice threatened to dislodge just above them, but they escaped this danger and reached the snowy plateau. Coleman described it as a scene "that was grand in the nakedness of its desolation." From their vantage point atop an icy wasteland, all around in the lowlands they could see red smoke from wildfires. Just below loomed the Black Buttes, rising above the haze of the depths, looking like fantastic ruins of giant cathedrals. They investigated the steaming crater, bare of snow, still awake after recent eruptions, awful in color and form, reeking of sulfur.

They succeeded in reaching camp after dark, with Coleman feeling the effects of fatigue and lagging behind. The dangers of being trapped in hostile, desolate terrain were lifted, and they were free to indulge in congratulations of reaching a goal. After much hard work, they had made a very brief visit to a magnificent vista where they could never feel at home. Coleman hints in his writings that he could not feel at home in the lowlands either; that before the trip he was "sick of the monotonous round of his ordinary occupation." But after this adventure, he could feel the exhilaration of renewal, and the resolve that the memory of these times would help overcome the ordinary drudgery of life.

Early explorers of the upper Nooksack soon found that the passes only led to more difficult terrain. After the snow has receded from winter's onslaught, one can make a more assured passage into the upper valleys, up Ruth Creek toward Hannegan Pass, still far from a crossing of the North Cascades. Most of the upper valley is a site of avalanche volleys, slopes where the normally prolific silver firs and mountain hemlocks only grow bent and prone, at best. Lingering spring snow allows easy passage over the soon-to-be-uncovered slide alder and a more difficult passage where the avalanche debris has thinned precariously over gushing side streams. Over the roar of Ruth Creek, the birds sing like crazy: the astonishing energetic song of the mouselike winter wren, the spring reveille of the fox sparrow. Big paw prints of a bear lead over the undulating and broken snow mounds and cross the creek to the forested slope where the trees have grown old where protected from slides. The warming temperatures, the reflectance from the snow of the increasingly strong sun, turn the recent snow to mush and threaten to topple the rock-hard cornices sculpted along the ridgelines.

There are times in the spring in the North Cascades when one might dance over the almost-sheer slopes, but taking an uncertain gully with broken conifers and evidence of slides everywhere and navigating around an overhanging cornice to the ridgetop may make one wonder. Across the deep chasm of the North Fork looms Mt. Shuksan, looking particularly fearsome now with its blank, dark walls loaded with downward-pointing snow slabs. Clouds in a static roil threaten to cover the fissured dome of Mt. Baker. The sun shines through a filmy, sullen sky. Not much time for comfort and self-complacency in such a place.

North wall of Mt. Shuksan, Nooksack Tower, Price Glacier

Mt. Baker and the buried slopes of Swift Creek

Baker

KULSHAN, AS THE LUMMI INDIAN TRIBE called Mt. Baker, has been remarkably quiet in the last century. More conical and less rived by glaciers than other Northwest volcanoes, it has remained in static repose, with a heavy mantle of habitual snow and long, fissured ice streams, while below, the frantic activity of civilization has commenced. Although there was some smoke and bellowing in 1975, that event passed without apparent significance. In the recent past, however, Mt. Baker has not always been so quiet. Up until about 1880, the mountain was spewing fire, and anything downstream from Boulder Creek and Sulphur Creek, including the Baker River and Skagit River, was in its path. There were a number of reports of eruptions that killed all the fish, including a particularly bad one in 1810 that wiped out the salmon run in the Skagit for two years.

Besides being altered by Baker's violent eruptions, the lower part of the Baker River has been altered by the Baker Lake Dam. But the upper part has remained virtually untouched, a deep chasm bounded by marvelous peaks such as Mt. Shuksan, extending deep within the jungly, trailless terrain below the Northern Picket Range. Above the lake, the valley floor is quite flat with opposing cliffs forested everywhere except where vertical or overhanging. In spring the river runs beautifully clear with emerald depths, within the broad, sandy flood channel, strewn with polished rocks, full of battered log debris. With the exception of extensive burns resulting from Mt. Baker's eruptions and intentional fires set by early settlers, fires do not normally occur, allowing long-standing, climax forests of western hemlocks, silver firs, and western red cedars. The cedars grow thick and huge, clustered along the valley sides away from the flood channel, sheltering mainly ferns in winter, a delicate ground cover in summer.

Clouds often draw down into the valley, spreading a drab mist, diffusing the distance, shutting out light from the depths of the forest. The rain falls steadily upon the lush carpet of vibrant, green moss that covers almost everything, growing thickly on tangles of vine maples, on trunks and boughs of big-leaf maples. The place is in constant flux, drenched with rain and runoff, under the shadow of Mt. Baker's eruptions, nurturing a riot of vegetation.

Of the men in the Cascades who spent the energy of their youth in hard labor, hacking the earth in search of freedom and a fortune, performing acts of prodigious physical strength in obscurity, one of the more legendary was Joe Morovits. In 1891, at a time when there were not any tree blazes, let alone trails, he established a solitary homestead some thirty-two miles within the dense forests of the Baker Valley. He used that location as a base for conducting mining operations another eight miles or more up the tenuous slopes of Swift Creek. Legend has it that he commonly hauled hundred-pound packs filled with all sorts of supplies including books and china, and somehow managed to drag literally tons of cable and cast-iron to a self-provisioned mill for crushing ore. He roamed the highlands between Mt. Baker and Mt. Shuksan in the company of mountain goats, patiently pounding out mines that yielded hardly anything, somewhere high amongst the mists and clouds and avalanches.

It is not difficult to see how he could have been inspired on those crisp, startlingly clear mornings when the day dawns and the pink rays from the east spread over the crevassed ice dome of Mt. Baker. He made a number of difficult ascents of Mt. Baker and perhaps one or more ascents of Mt. Shuksan; at first, with all the trappings and enthusiasm of a rank novice, such as the time when he carried a rifle while pioneering a route up the Boulder Glacier. But being inspired on those magnificent mountain days is one thing and enduring the cold, dark rainy season is another. As the summer days die away, an almost invincible pall of gray spreads over the land, and the sun's nourishing influence departs. How did he manage during those long nights before electricity when there was only that stark simplicity of staring into a fire, listening to the endless rain beat monotonous rhythms on the carefully cut cedar planks? He continued his quest for twenty-seven years, far beyond the point where success or failure had any meaning. Being out there in the wilds of the Baker Valley, fighting and living with the elements, had become a way of life.

In winter, the snow falls with a seemingly endless predictability over the high country. The driving flakes and dense clouds make a white blindness for anyone crazy enough to venture out during the short daylight hours. But occasionally, the skies clear to a deep, frigid blue and the sun shines its diminished light over the buried slopes. The air can be quite still and brittle during these intervals, and the soft snow crystals glint prismatic colors in the sunshine. Above Swift Creek, along the ridge from Table Mountain, the enduring mountain hemlocks stand as ghostly forms clumped together on the ridge, rigid in thick coats of rime ice, set against a scenic backdrop of the pure-white dome of Mt. Baker and the precipitous snow- and ice-plastered cliffs of Mt. Shuksan. Only the ravens are active: emitting their weird, nasal calls as they flap their shadowy wings in a survey of the empty, snowy expanses. The light turns golden, then rosy, and fades as it touches only the higher reaches, the cold beauty of Shuksan.

Western hemlocks and vine maples along Baker Lake

Heather blooms, Anderson Lakes, Mt. Baker

Spring runoff down Diobsub Creek

TODAY, IN THE COMFORT OF OUR AUTOMOBILES we can whiz up the North Cascades Highway, along Gorge and Diablo Lakes. As we make a stop to view the violent crashing of water through the deep, airy chasm of Gorge Creek, amidst our physical ease we can try to envision what it might have been like to be a miner venturing into Ruby Creek or Thunder Creek by this route a century ago. Before the Gorge Dam was built, miners hauled their cast-iron equipment with horses and mules along a perilous path, the "goat trail," blasted into the rock face. Imagine what it would be like during the long summer days when the heat brought out multitudes of stinging deer flies; or in late fall during the drenching, cold rains; or in winter when the deep, heavy snows triggered deadly avalanches.

The development of the upper Skagit River was initiated by prospectors and miners in search of riches within the earth. They were fortune-seekers who, if they were not at the time of their arrival, had to develop into strong individualists. In addition to the wearing grind of hard labor, they had to suffer the heartache of seeing their visions of success yield only a grudging subsistence at best. Despite the exorbitant claims of riches in the mountains, very few profitable mining ventures ever resulted despite all the trouble and effort. A few, such as John MacMillian, George Holmes, and Tom Rowland, stayed in the upper valley and established homesteads in the days before the river was dammed. In a memoir, Will Jenkins writes of fond recollections of MacMillian and Holmes, whom he knew personally as a youth. A Canadian by birth, John MacMillian abandoned claims along the Fraser River and moved up the Skagit in 1883. In the days before the lower Big Beaver Valley was flooded, he established a homestead among giant cedars and the roar of the old river. Holmes was a remarkably independent man who was born a slave in Virginia in 1854. By an abiding strength and persistence, he was one of the few miners who, when all was said and done, managed to make a profit.

Of all the mining ventures up the Skagit River, one of the more grandiose was the one conducted by the Skagit Queen Mining Company. Once the travail of leading the horses and mules up the Skagit Gorge was completed, this enterprise involved crossing the waters of the deep glacial drainage Thunder Creek and then continuing some fifteen miles south through a deeply cut valley, up the headwaters of Skagit Queen Creek to the Boston Glacier, a huge amphitheater of falling ice set below the arc of peaks from Buckner to Boston to Forbidden. Today, out of the thick carpets of moss that cover a boulder field near the mouth of Skagit Queen Creek extend the rusted pipes once linked to compressor drills in the mine, somewhere high above the jungly valley. The vein, which adventurous prospectors found in a daring trek over the Boston Glacier, turned out to be no more than a surface deposit.

The pioneers had great difficulty with the fluctuating water levels of the river. The construction of hydroelectric dams by Seattle City Light stabilized the flow of runoff and converted the wildly rushing water into a public resource. Besides that, the dams provided three magnificent glacial-fed lakes that are scenic and recreational treasures. But the benefits have not come without loss.

As part of a summer of intense journeying to map the 49th parallel (the current United States and Canadian border), in 1859 Henry Custer followed an overland route to the upper Skagit River. After a few day's rest from venturing over hill and dale of the Chilliwack drainage, in early August Custer started from the beautiful expanse of Chilliwack Lake with two white companions and a contingent of seven Indians. The trail soon disappeared near the border and his party bushwhacked through beautiful and rugged, unknown territory. Custer had by this time become well accustomed to the dense valley tangles of vine maple and slide alder, with their wicked branches that are bent by the heavy winter snowpack and tend to grow horizontally. Since these branches usually grow higher than the height of a human, progress is only made by hacking them with a machete or by the most insistent, painstaking effort, in which one often finds oneself either whiplashed or spread-eagled off the ground. Other obstacles, once one has disentangled from the alder thickets, are the bogs, rife in midsummer with two stinging nuisances: devil's club, which is at least stationary, and the mosquito.

After an interminable effort, a traveler may easily be discouraged by a lack of progress, looking up at the peaks, now awesomely remote. But Custer kept going all summer, drawn by the mystique of the North Cascades, by the hidden and wild beauty, requiring much trouble and effort just to approach. The hard, continuous effort of alternately dropping into the valley jungles and then panting and puffing to high points was easily justified:

> *"Nowhere do the mountain masses and peaks present such strange, fantastic, dauntless, and startling outlines as here. Whoever wishes to see Nature in all its primitive glory and grandeur, in its almost ferocious wildness, must go and visit these Mountain regions."*

From the top of Easy Ridge, they surveyed their route to the Skagit and made a wonderful camp on a rarefied subalpine meadow beside a sky reflecting pool, among granite boulders, heather and huckleberry, and stunted firs. They saw many signs of mountain goats and ran into two small flocks of them. Of the large mammals, only mountain goats have the nerve to brave the precarious winter conditions of the North Cascades. In the deep, heavy snow where every down-sloping glacier basin is an avalanche trap, it is a wonder that any survive. The travelers took the deep drop into Brush Creek, crossed the divide at Whatcom Pass, and marveled at the icy extent of the Challenger Glacier—certainly more spectacular and of greater size during the mini-ice age of the nineteenth century.

> *"Nothing ever seen before could compare to the matchless grandeur of this feature in nature. Imagine the Niagara Falls tens of times magnified in height and size, and this vast sheet of water instantly crystallized and rendered permanently solid, and you have a somewhat adequate idea of the immensity of this natural phenomena."*

Clutching onto roots, they dropped into the Little Beaver Creek Valley, alternately hacking their way through the choking brush and taking the track of the glacier-fed streambed, the water colored a distinct dark blue from the suspended glacial particles. As their food stocks ran low and the skies grew threatening, eliciting some concern, they came upon the Skagit River (where Ross Lake now stands), which appeared as a clear stream about 50 to 60 yards wide, running almost directly south. The Indians built canoes and they followed the river's course, portaging past dense clots of logs and running past obstacles of diverging channels. They fished for "brown speckled trout," which was plentiful where the waters were deep and the current slow. The valley narrowed near the Big Beaver outlet, and they ran the rapids with increasing trepidation. As Custer noted that everyone was on edge, he halted their river run just before a plunge into a lower section of the gorge. They had almost reached the convergence of Ruby Creek, another narrowly hewn rock gorge. Some years later, in 1878, a prospector named Jack Rowley would have a dream and point in the direction of Ruby Creek as a place to find gold. Long after the ensuing stampede, George Holmes could be found in that vicinity, patiently working his claim for forty-one years.

Today, a trail makes travel on Custer's route considerably easier, and the North Cascades Highway obviates the grueling pull up the Skagit Gorge; but the surrounding mountains and drainages are no less rugged and wild. The Picket Range and the Challenger Glacier, which Custer marveled at, still retain their remote beauty and wilderness mystique. Because of the difficulty of access, a visit to these remote areas still requires extended time and effort. And, the weather holds the same uncertainty. Hardly ever is it guaranteed that the skies will not close and envelope the peaks for long periods.

Much of the interior land of the Skagit watershed remains roadless, even trailless, and is now preserved in North Cascades National Park. The fervor of the miners has long since died, and logging interests have never established strong claims in this precipitous territory. The Park Service did have development plans for the newly created national park. One planned project involved building a tramway from Ross Lake, where it could be accessible by motorboat, up Arctic Creek to an overlook of the North Cascade heartland. But, in 1988 the area was given wilderness status, and such Swiss-like development projects were abandoned.

Henry Custer's view of the Challenger Glacier many years later

The Southern Pickets and the depths of Goodell Creek

Boston Glacier from the alder thickets of the Skagit Queen Valley

Cedar, Pacific silver fir, and western hemlock forest, Kindy Creek

Cascade

In April the lower reaches of the Cascade River come alive from their winter slumber. The damp, heavy air gives way to soft breezes and the heartening warmth of the sun's rays. The days grow noticeably longer and birds such as the winter wren ring the air with the energy of a new season. In the old forests of western hemlock and red cedar, the first flowers of the season, such as trilliums and yellow violets, sprout on the moss-carpeted duff. In the lower reaches of the roaring tributaries, set in a protected nook beneath a waterfall and along a wreckage of battered logs, perhaps a few astonishingly large steelhead trout may still be seen swimming in an emerald pool.

The current Cascade River road started as an Indian route, crossing Cascade Pass, and arriving east of the crest in the valley of the Stehekin. Miners used this Indian route in the late nineteenth century to chase their dreams, into the glaciated mountains above and beyond Cascade Pass. There were big plans to build a trans-mountain road at about this time of furious mining activity, but it was never linked to the east side. In 1897, with funding from the State of Washington, the "Cascade Wagon Road" was constructed to the twelve-mile mark (near Sibley Creek), and in the same year it was almost thoroughly washed away by floods. Today, the forest service road, which annually requires repairs from washouts and avalanche debris, extends up the North Fork, below the crashing icefalls of the north face of Mt. Johannesberg, where it provides access to the popular Cascade Pass Trail.

In general, anyone venturing far up the deep, glacially carved and water-pounded valleys in the North Cascades anywhere off the beaten track should be wished a lot of luck. Trails not maintained disappear rapidly, taken over by stinging brush or downed trees or stream outwashes. Nearly impenetrable alder and vine maple thickets can be counted upon to choke the avalanche tracks and trailing. The heavy snowpack during the long winters causes frequent slides, snapping and splintering the tough conifers, making cross-country travel deep within the valleys extremely hazardous. The best bet for reaching the upper valleys is during the late spring when the deep snows moderate but still cover the lower slopes. Another time to make the approach is late summer after the gushing snowmelt subsides, when it becomes feasible to hike up the streambeds, over the banks of bare glacial rubble.

Backcountry travelers can explore the less well-trodden reaches of the Cascade River by taking an indistinct spur road and bumping past the latest outwashes and fallen tree snags. Old cedars still thrive within the deep, shadowed valley where the trail nearly parallels the glacial-silted Cascade River. The Middle Fork Trail rises rapidly above a thundering waterfall on a steep, moss-clad, boulder slope where large Douglas firs grow due to the greater sun exposure. As the trail levels out, the sidewalls of the canyon grow precipitous and block out a considerable amount of sunlight. As in many of these shadowy valleys, old silver firs and hemlocks grow with a predominant understory of sour huckleberry. Once beyond the reach of easy access, some pleasant and secluded campsites can be found close to crystal-clear streams. Rusting mining debris occasionally lines the creekbed or lies forgotten among the thick vegetation, the last vestiges of hard labor, bare subsistence, and visions of wealth. Where the trail breaks from the forest, barbed berry vines and the sprawling, entangling alders thrive in dense jungles that grow above head level in summer.

With any kind of threat of rain, a wise course of action is to make camp and reassess, for the reason that anyone doing any kind of bushwhacking when it rains will get thoroughly soaked. After a night out in a secluded valley, a perfect haven for black bears, the traveler may be heartened to continue even in less than propitious weather. The best way to reach the head of the valley is by hopping the boulders; tracing the violent action on the streambeds, wading through the icy water of the Middle Fork, at least until the alder hell can be left behind. From there, its mostly uphill through a narrowing glacier-cut gorge, at first on open rocky moraines, home of marmots and pikas, and then onto firn and ice and a jumble of boulders. Still well below timberline, most plants by this time are left behind at this elevation below 5,000 feet. A long ridgeline extends west with open slopes of stunted firs and meadows, a favorite habitat of mountain goats. Though well out of the range from danger, they are shy and elusive and will probably make their way out of sight. Ahead loom the rough, weathered walls of Mt. Formidible and the cracked and fissured blue ice in a frozen tumble down the Formidible and Middle Cascade Glaciers.

The illusion of solid permanence starts to crack as one goes higher up the rock and ice to more precarious holds above screaming depths. The immense natural forces create an awe-inspiring presence and sense of flux: the groaning of the thick, cracked sheet of ice; the crashing of a loose rock down a rubbly, broken gully; the hard wind that blows cold mist and clouds over the vertical rock wall. These mountains have not been here forever and they, like all mountains, are in a process of being worn down and changed irrevocably. Yet, next summer they will be nearly the same, as well as the following summer, as well as all the brief summers of a lifetime. From clues gathered from the rocks one can surmise: against the backdrop of geological time, it was not long ago at all when this place was not at all the same as today. Sediments, laid down many millions of years ago in faraway seas, comprising islands or sub-continents off the Northwest, collided and fused along the Northwest coast. Great pressures within the earth's crust resulted in folding and faulting, which metamorphosed the rock into the crystalline core of the North Cascades and lifted it. Then, rivers of ice gnawed on its great flanks through ages of wintery, frigid shadows.

Middle Cascade Glacier on Mt. Formidable

Ridge running to El Dorado, granite on Hidden Lake Peak

Spring waterfall above Goat Lake, upper Sauk

Sauk

FROM THE NINETEENTH-CENTURY MINING CLAIMS along Silver Creek, above the North Fork of the Skykomish, it took some heart and initiative to venture from the lowland brush into the unknown highlands to the north. None of the adventurous fortune-seekers who filed mining claims along Silver Creek as early as 1874 climbed into those northern hills or at least made a big deal out of it until Joseph Pearsall did in 1889. Pearsall brought back ore samples from what he perceived to be a mountain of galena, the sulphide ore of lead, which often contains significant amounts of silver. Pearsall was accompanied on subsequent explorations that summer by another miner, Frank Peabody, and at least one of the Wilmans brothers, who were investors. During their investigation they dropped into '76 Gulch and climbed to a saddle above Glacier Basin, where they contoured across Wilman's Glacier. They came to the astonishing conclusion that the vein of galena in '76 Gulch extended all the way through the ridge to the other side of Glacier Basin, an incredible discovery. Totally exhilarated and fired by visions of wealth, they continued explorations to the confluence of '76 Creek and Glacier Creek.

They did not know it at the time, but they had also discovered the headwaters of the Sauk River. Upon returning, Pearsall and Peabody decided to follow the river's course, rather than return by way of Silver Creek. They had already been out for several days and their provisions were low, but they were still soaring from their discovery. In taking the long northward course along the Sauk, they found it unnervingly brushy with very little evidence of previous human presence. They probably came upon faint Indian trails, perhaps previous encampments, but they found nothing to alleviate their hunger for seven days until they wandered far beyond the present town of Darrington and reached a farmhouse some nine miles from the Skagit River.

A town named Monte Cristo, with a population exceeding 1,000 during its heyday, was built far within the jungly valleys and underneath glaciated peaks on the basis of Pearsall's discovery. It took some thirty years (1890–1920), through depression years and times of prosperity, to convince commercial interests that the rich vein of galena was mostly a surface deposit; that the more they drilled (and they drilled for years and years through miles of tunnels) the less profitable was the ore.

Like other westside watersheds the climate in this area provides a tremendous amount of moisture through the winter months. Inevitably, the heavy snow would load the bowls below the peaks, and the result would be disastrous avalanches that would wipe out trams, edifices, posing a great risk to the miners. Any structure in town had to be maintained throughout the winter, otherwise it would be found crushed by the weight of the snow the following spring. When the railroad could not operate, which was frequent despite the wonders of clearing the deep, heavy snow by a rotary plow, the town was cut off from supplies save what could be snowshoed fourteen miles in from Silverton. Then there were the floods, which on occasion caused great damage.

After the startling clarity and deep blue skies of autumn, which are an emphatic finale to the benign days of summer, darkening clouds bring deluges of cold rain and a deep snowpack, which in combination with the steep gradients and unstable glacial soils, can cause violent erosion. Since the last Ice Age, the long-standing forests, the kind that develop multi-layered canopies and thick carpets of moss and duff after centuries of uninterrupted growth, have made a definite difference in mitigating raging floodwaters. Old silver firs and western hemlocks, which are perfectly suited to the cold dampness of the upper valleys, can hold an enormous amount of snow, as any cross-country winter wanderer can attest during a windstorm. Eventually, the heavily laden boughs lose their loads by wind or rain or melting. When the heavy rains come, besides the factor of the thick vegetation that is much better at holding the moisture than bare slopes, there is simply less of a snowpack than in the open.

The two major tributaries of the Sauk, the Suiattle River and the Whitechuck River, form deeply forested, curved valleys that virtually encircle and drain the entire Glacier Peak area. Like Mt. St. Helens and the old Mt. Mazama (now Crater Lake), Glacier Peak has rained plenty of pumice in faraway places. Unlike the volcanoes of the Oregon Cascades, Glacier Peak does not stand in splendid isolation along the Cascade Crest. From closer vantage points it makes a very singular appearance, such as from Image Lake and Buck Creek Pass. But, perhaps its most characteristic aspect is how it towers above a wild array of glaciated peaks, which seem to surround it from most every angle. During the summer months, when the glaciers melt, the lower Sauk often takes on a cloudy turquoise or a muddy brown appearance in its lower reaches, due to the grinding of Glacier Peak's glaciers and the crumbling debris slopes.

The Sauk, for a time, was a last refuge of the Indians who once roamed freely up the valleys. Nels Bruseth, a devoted forest ranger from the town of Darrington, reported that the stature of these mountain Indians was taller and hardier than the Sound Indians, and that they had a richer collection of legends and tales. An established overland travel route up the North Fork over a pass called Indian Pass allowed intermingling between the Wenatchee bands and the Sauk bands. There were reports that in the past they used the brushy valley of Sulphur Creek (a tributary of the Suiattle River) to cross Kaiwhat Pass, into Brush Creek and into the Agnes River Valley to Lake Chelan.

When D. C. (Daniel Chapman) Linsley made railroad surveys up the Sauk in 1870, he relied on the natives for direction, finding their information about the terrain reliable. Linsley was charged with finding a feasible railroad pass through the North Cascades to Lake Chelan and the Columbia River. He, together with John Tennant (who accompanied Edmund Coleman in the first ascent of Mt. Baker), made extensive investigations of the long and deeply forested valleys between May and July. Linsley approached such obstacles as dangerous high water, incessant cold rain, dwindling provisions, being alone with natives with whom he did not share the same language or customs, and traveling through deep slushy snow with a business-like ruthlessness. Considering the difficulties of hacking through the overgrown tangles of Sulphur Creek in a day before there were any easy approach routes, Linsley's journals are full of understatement, mainly focusing on the contours of the valleys as they relate to the feasibility of a railroad route. The Indians objected to traveling such a route, thinking it too difficult, and staged a protest, but Linsley's sense of duty was strong enough to persuade them and to see for himself the impracticality of traversing the upper Suiattle to Lake Chelan.

Linsley related that during the heyday of fur-trading, Sulphur Creek was an established route that the Indians used to reach Fort Okanogan to the east, but since that time it had been virtually abandoned. There was a faint trail along the Suiattle, but once they reached the mouth of Sulphur Creek, they were on their own. It took them two hard-fought days to reach the head of the valley. They found the characteristic wonders of North Cascades valleys: the huge cedars, the bears that love the upper reaches, the pounding waterfalls, the deep precipitous slopes culminating in stupendous glaciated mountains such as Dome Peak. They were lucky that they had chosen early June to make the trip; otherwise, they would have had to fight more brush. After spending a day reconnoitering the pass, Linsley concluded that only a tunnel in this remote, out-of-the-way place would make a rail line possible. On their way back they pushed themselves to exhaustion through the trailless brush and past streams gushing with runoff to the place where they had left the canoes. From there, Linsley found himself whirling down the raging, swollen river in canoes piloted by expert Indian paddlers, barely missing large glacial boulders and stranded log debris.

Linsley was not anywhere close to being finished at that point. He made further explorations up the Sauk watershed, following the Indian trail up the North Fork of the Sauk to the more well traveled Indian Pass, this time encountering a different ordeal: long dismal days of constant, cold rain. There were more such days along with the eastside sun, as he crossed into the Wenatchee drainage and then returned by way of the Columbia River, Lake Chelan, the Stehekin, Agnes Creek, and Spruce Creek, nearly all the way back to Kaiwhat Pass from the east.

Cedar, Pacific silver fir, and western hemlock forest above the Whitechuck River

Glacier Peak from Circle Mountain

Moss bed in Gothic Basin

Chelan-Sawtooth Mountains from the Upper Twisp Valley

Methow

THE HYDROLOGIC DIVIDE OF THE CASCADES veers almost directly eastward (some 18 to 20 miles) from Cascade Pass to Washington Pass, and then traces a fairly northerly line to Canada. The Skagit River watershed is so large that it bulges east of the usual crest, well beyond Ross Lake into the Pasayten Wilderness. The Methow River drains the drier highlands east of the Skagit watershed and the Chelan highlands, and flows south into the Columbia. Its prominent tributaries include the Lost River and Chewuch River, which originate amidst the long ridges and ice-gouged cirques of the Pasayten, trending toward lands that support a more boreal type ecosystem, habitat of moose and lynx. Other tributaries, such as the Twisp River, drain the Chelan highlands.

The landscape reveals the cumulative effects of the Pleistocene Epoch, the repeated advances and retreats of rivers of ice that began not so long ago in geological time□some two million years ago. In this almost unimaginably extended history of the ebb and flow of ice, the most recent advance reached its maximum only some 15,000 years ago. During this latest advance (while the site of the city of Seattle was covered by over 3,000 feet of ice), most of the Methow area was at one time or another inundated by a lobe of the great Cordilleran ice sheet. Landforms of the Methow were submerged under this sheet of ice, as can be inferred from the rounding of ridgetops and high points. Only intermittent jagged rock forms protruded, as in the case of the headwaters of Early Winters Creek.

Early Winters Creek originates just below Washington Pass in a land of pointed and sharply hewn granite spires. Only the barest of remnants of the glaciers remain on the north side of Silver Star Mountain, small remains of the downward ice action that cleaved, sculpted, and hacked the raw, ancient rock that rises high now in vertical precipices, orange and dark stained, lichen encrusted. Steep gullies send the season□s snow and rock debris careening into the valley in wide avalanche fans, pushing against the encroaching conifers deep in the dark, green valley. In spring, the creek roars down its rock-cluttered channel, swollen from the runoff. In the lower reaches grow more sun-tolerant trees such as ponderosa pines and aspens, both beautiful and distinctive. Soon the hot sun will sear the slopes, but for now the lush, green folds are dappled with cheery, yellow arrowleaf balsamroot flowers. A tender, green ground cover grows in the wake of the retreating snow through the soft pine needles.

The bare rock highlands of the Pasayten rival the westerly North Cascades in height but are now almost totally devoid of glaciers. Winter snows disappear fast under the glaring heat of the sun. Thunderstorms roar over the arid ridgetops in summer, but the dark, forbidding clouds seldom bring much refreshment. Mostly they bring lightning strikes that blacken and char the Douglas firs and pines that grow widely spaced in the rocky granitic soil amidst the dry fragrance of sticky, leathery snowbrush bushes. Lost River and Eureka Creek cut through deeply excavated chasms, almost a mile in depth, their shimmering crystalline waters usually unreachable to the wearied high country traveler. The ridges are reminiscent of the Rocky Mountains, where whitebark pines grow with their scaly ashen bark that often gets ripped, revealing the heartwood that grows in a spiral, burnished tawny and amber.

In resisting the harsh whims of the elements, no tree comes close to matching alpine larches. They grow high on the rocky crags, such as Silver Star, in the barest of soils, always selecting the especially cold northerly slopes, far above where other higher elevation trees, such as the subalpine fir and whitebark pine, have long since disappeared. They insist upon growing upright, resisting the rigors of blasting storms, leafless and bare during the cold and dark winters, in summer decked with bright green needles, looking very much like a typical conifer. They retain their greenery only through the summer. Early in the fall, they are transformed into a flaming golden orange in the waning sunlight.

When Alexander Ross wandered west in 1814 from his fur trader's outpost of Fort Okanogan, he found very little evidence of previous human activity. He was told by his Indian guides of the trade route which crossed the North Cascades, but as he started on that route up the Methow, he reported few signs that anyone had preceded him, just a "pathless desert" along the Methow or the nearly "impervious" forest up the valleys. He learned that the eastern tribes traded such items as hemp, a durable material that the westside tribes used for fishing nets, in exchange for maritime items that were more ornamental than anything else. But if there was a road or path for that trade, Ross did not see one, even though he was being guided by one who knew the way.

In 1882, when Henry Pierce led an Army expedition through the same territory, the valley had changed very little, although Pierce found a well-defined trail to follow. He ran into several Chelan natives but did not see any signs of settlement, or at least did not report them. He only described the beautiful natural setting of a broad valley of bunch grass bounded by benches of pine and fir and snow-capped peaks, with the crystalline waters of the Methow River flowing through a winding channel of shady trees.

Ponderosa pines along Foggy Dew Creek

Alpine Larch above the Chewuch drainage

White Rock Lakes, West Fork of the Agnes

Stehekin

THE GLACIAL ACTION ON THE EAST SIDE OF CASCADE PASS has also cut dramatic features, even more so when considering Lake Chelan. The contrast between the roughly sculpted ice peaks and the deep, green valleys is no less stirring than the west side. More than 10,000 years ago frozen rivers descended what are now the major tributaries of Agnes Creek, Bridge Creek, and Park Creek, uniting in the Stehekin, forming an excavating force that carved out the fifty-five miles of the current Lake Chelan, digging into the bedrock 436 feet below sea level, the deepest part of the lake. Today, the glaciers have retreated to mere remnants, and what remains are the deep valleys, including the Stehekin, "the way through," and the beautiful long water expanse of Lake Chelan.

Alexander Ross, who made the first crossing of the Cascades by a European in 1814, was not very explicit about his route, but he was traveling in a rugged, uncalculated wilderness. From Ross's sketchy descriptions, his compass readings, and knowledge of the Indian routes that crossed the Cascades, it's probable Ross traveled up the Twisp River, crossed Copper Pass, hacked his way down Bridge Creek, and then followed the Stehekin on his way to crossing the crest at Cascade Pass. Ross had a strong spirit of independence in venturing into the heart of the North Cascades long before any other European would follow his footsteps. Traveling under a persistent gloomy cloud cover, he complained that the forests were "almost impervious" and "A more difficult route to travel never fell to man's lot." He carried only meager provisions, depending on his own means for sustenance.

The way along the Stehekin could hardly have been more than a faint path, as the Indians made no organized construction efforts. By midsummer, toward the upper valley where the steep, side slopes avalanche deep and heavy snow for much of the year, most of the valley floor is covered by a nearly impassable riot of undergrowth. Slide alder, vine maples, willow, and assorted brambles grow above head level. Today, a beaten path, well maintained by chain saws and a constant pounding of boots, provides a luxurious way compared to what Ross must have faced. Big blocks of veined and banded gneiss get ripped away from the steep walls, forming sharp, splintered talus; at least here there is no vegetation. The valley culminates in the steep wall of a hanging valley, Pelton Basin, which contains stately old mountain hemlocks a safe distance from the winter avalanche volleys from Magic Mountain and Sahale Arm.

Despite the enervating obstacles, Ross seems to have managed to reach Cascade Pass in one day from Bridge Creek. In apparently crossing to the west side, the unexpected arose, as he and his Indian companions ran into an incredible storm:

> "If I could compare it to anything, it would be to the rush of a heavy body of water, falling from a height; but when it came down opposite to where we stood, in a moment we beheld the woods before it bending down like grass before the scythe! It was the wind, accompanied by a torrent of rain—a perfect hurricane, such as I had never witnessed before."

Ross was a fiercely practical man who was ambitious, career-minded, and worked for the extremely status-conscious British Northwest Fur Company. It would be in his nature to wonder about the natives: Why, even though they had made trips across the mountains in order to trade, were they not enterprising enough to establish more assurance of the way? He called them "the great nabobs of the Cascades." All of Ross's efforts were trained to eliminate the uncertainty and mystery of the wilderness and to encourage ordinary habits, those habits that promoted business, the ledger of profit and loss. When his companions wavered because of the unknowns of the journey or fears upon confronting this freak storm, which due to their isolated condition must have seemed no less than supernatural, he had very critical things to say about them. But the natives had very little interest in attaching the ordinary and mundane to mountain places. To them, the mountain wilderness remained a realm of spirits and awesome mystery. Interestingly enough, when it came time for Ross to continue west without a guide, he drew the line of his independence; and in fact, admitted anxiety and went back the way he had come when faced with the uncertainties of going ahead alone.

After Ross came prospectors scratching their way into the mountains, leaving very little trace of their struggles, at least until the 1890s when a road part way up the Stehekin allowed them to haul their incredibly heavy cast-iron implements into the avalanche hazard of Horseshoe Basin and elsewhere. In 1882, an Army expedition headed by Henry Pierce retraced Ross's route up the Stehekin. Contrary to earlier explorers such as Ross or Henry Custer, Pierce did not travel with a contingent of native guides, although he relied heavily for direction on a man of Indian descent named LaFleur. Pierce was part of a several-decades-long effort to find a feasible mountain pass to Puget Sound, and like other explorers of this time, he considered that no one had come before him. Unlike Custer who was careful to discover and relate the native place names, Pierce named outstanding features of the landscape after himself and his friends.

After starting at the Okanogan, Pierce entered the Stehekin Valley by way of War Creek, where he chanced upon an old miner and a younger companion in a ragtag, sunburned state but still clinging to dreams of finding riches. Pierce's group took a difficult route, with some disastrous results to their mules, to Purple Pass and then down the long, steep drop (some 6,000 feet) to the upper edge of Lake Chelan. It seems they had relatively little trouble traveling the lower Stehekin due to the open eastside, boulder-cluttered forest of mostly Douglas firs. He described how the river here was full of trout averaging about a pound and that they frequently heard rattlesnakes. The going got considerably more difficult farther up the valley where the wetter climate encourages jungles of undergrowth. Pierce noted a crude bridge of drift logs, cedar strips, and boulders over Bridge Creek, a rare construction in the mountains at that time.

As they clambered over the sharp, splintered rocks above their camp at Horseshoe Basin Creek, they chanced upon the old miner again, this time warning them in the manner of some ghostly prophet that they and their stock would never make it over Cascade Pass. Dark clouds and mist had closed in over the treacherous rock and ice of Magic Mountain, and a hard sleet blew in their faces. An advance party spent an uncomfortable night in the desolate Pelton Basin, huddled around a campfire without a tent, noting the ominous booms from avalanches in between shivering in front of the fire. The next day they realized the futility of dragging their mules up the slippery, saturated vegetation along the steep cliffs, and split the group in order to continue without them. They still had a long way to go down what appeared to be a foreboding, questionably passable valley. But it was not long before the skies cleared, allowing an open view of the hacked pinnacles of the Triplets, the crashing glaciers on Mt. Johannesberg, and the green depths of the Cascade River, a magnificent view that would hearten any willing explorer.

The tributaries of the Stehekin, such as the West Fork of the Agnes, Park Creek and Flat Creek, cut into deep-forested valleys that drop precipitously from the glaciated cirques of the crest. To take the trail up Flat Creek is to leave behind today's well-traveled gravel road of the Stehekin for the less assured, the less pedestrian. The trail leads through the usual open avalanched areas, which need to be cleared every summer, with distant views of the ice and rock of LaConte and Sentinel. Then it dips toward the flood channel of the creek into a forest of huge, tapering trunks of western red cedars. On a blustery summer's eve when storm clouds billow up over the crest and break into the blue, swallows can sometimes be seen slicing through the air with long glides and swoops. The trail goes nowhere from here. The stream splits into several rushing watercourses along banks of glacial rubble choked with the usual North Cascades brush, shutting off easy passage, beckoning all the same.

White Rock Lakes, West Fork of the Agnes

Chiwaukum Mountains from Nason Ridge

Wenatchee/Entiat

AFTER THE NUMBING DARKNESS OF THE LONG NIGHTS OF WINTER, for a very brief time the highlands of the Cascades come alive in a celebration of life. Though the ridge crests in the Glacier Peak area never rise any higher than the bare ridges of the Pasayten, snow may cover most of the higher hills until well into August. But the snowbanks disappear as the sun burns over the profuse flower meadows, the lush vibrant green grass and translucent huckleberry, the hearty conifers stretching their supple limbs. Night falls from a hushed twilight with a flush of crimson and rainbow colors receding to the west. After a short, warm night with an infinity of stars, incredibly distant yet somehow close to a youthful audience, morning dawns like magic, with a renewal of hope and a fresh outlook.

The deep glacially carved valleys of the Little Wenatchee, Indian Creek, White River, Napeequa River, Chiwawa River, Icicle Creek, Ingalls Creek, and Entiat River extend for long, roadless distances on the eastside of the crest. Today, trails provide long approaches that both tax and inspire the enthusiastic wanderer, jarred away from another world of traffic jams and hectic decisions, intent upon shunning the stifling comforts and habits of everyday town life for the long trek to lush flower gardens and the desolation of magnificent peaks.

Upper eastside valleys, such as the Little Wenatchee, have a definite wet, westside character, receiving a heavy winter snowpack extremely prone to avalanching. Traversing the sun filled, open obstacle course of winter's ravaged slopes is a price to be paid for reaching the all-too-brief bloom of beauty of the highlands. Cluttered with downed logs, choked with summer ferns, slide alder, and assorted brambles that in concert grow above head level, the trail usually does not provide smooth sailing. The hotter it gets the worse the flies: they attack kamikaze style, sure to find a mark, ferocious compared with the decorous hovering of mosquitoes. If it were not for the treacherous winter slides, silver firs and western hemlock, the most prolific of North Cascades trees, would grow just about everywhere not strictly vertical. During hot, oppressive summer afternoons, they provide a cool respite from the brushy, fly-ridden open spaces.

Away from the crest, moving farther east, the vegetation grows increasingly sparse and brittle in the drier climate. The summer sun burns all the moisture out of ponderosa pine snags and dead underbrush. The extensive lower Wenatchee river system, including Tumwater Canyon, the Chiwaukam drainages, Icicle Creek, and Ingalls Creek, all deep valleys carved out of crystalline rock, have seen their lower slopes regularly charred by summer blazes. In 1994 wildfires of an enormous scale swept into Tumwater Canyon and Icicle Creek, and especially through the lower Entiat. Strong winds whipped firestorms that overwhelmed vast tracts of trees, leaving behind a thick layer of gray ash.

The conflagration of the eastside valleys or the glory of the meadows along the crest, events of summer, last for a very brief time. The bright, nodding lilies give way to purple lupines, and then the meadows lose their freshness and life. As August comes to an end, after the heat and light of the long days, the rank meadows start to take on an air of abandonment, as if the long-awaited festival is drawing to a close and most of the celebrants have left. The air starts to have a bite then; darkness comes earlier; seed pods rustle with a brittle sound; and there is that piercing, bittersweet scent of dying flowers and annuals.

As the sun loses its strength and the meadows turn a dull brown, the basins take on an empty expanse, devoid now of cheery birdsongs and burgeoning, green growth. The highlands of the Entiat and Wenatchee take on the chilling, lonely aspect of bare, inanimate rocks and a tremendous silence. There is a lot less assurance now in wondering the higher hills, especially when dark clouds bring snow and a forbidding cold. At one time in the not-too-distant past, no one had calculated distances or drew maps to assure locations. There was more mystery then and more of the ultimate in the waning, brilliant days leading to winter.

The Entiat drainage parallels Lake Chelan and the Stehekin River but does not extend to the crest. It culminates at the steep walls of Mt. Maude and Seven Fingered Jack, which form a jagged boundary with the Chiwawa and Railroad Creek. An explorer, venturing up the Entiat before the sheepherders turned loose their flocks and the loggers built roads and cut swaths in the forests, would have started from the arid, bare volcanic rock above the Columbia. The natives would have worn paths up the lower part of the valley, especially to the advantageous fishing spots where the salmon could be speared from banks of lush spring grasses under the shade of cottonwoods. The paths could hardly have been frequent since there was comparatively little settlement or enterprise by the few nomadic tribes. Away from the river on the sun-blazed slopes and hollows, cross-country travel would not have been a problem through the glades, the widely spaced ponderosa pines, often charred from summer fires. Farther up, the valley deepens from past glacial action through the crystalline rock, and the Douglas firs become more prominent, mingling with pines and aspens. Where avalanche tracts start appearing with resulting grassy meadows, aspens stand bravely in their wakes.

A time to wander through the remote upper forests of the Entiat to the high country is in June or early summer just before dusk, when the brilliance of the summer light softens into twilight. Two of the greatest songsters of the wilderness, the Swainson thrush and Hermit thrush, can be heard then. In the stillness of the darkening forest, as the day seeps away, their songs echo with exquisite fluting, lone voices against a backdrop of awesome silence and wilderness solitude.

The granite of Mt. Stuart and the serpentine of Ingalls Lake

Penstemon, North Fork of the Entiat

Mt. Saska from Fern Lake, North Fork of the Entiat

Vine maples, South Fork of the Stillaguamish

Stillaguamish

THE FOUNTAINS OF THE STILLAGUAMISH do not originate anywhere along the current Cascade Crest. There is strong evidence that at one time the original headwaters of both the North and South Forks changed course and were diverted into what is now the northward-flowing Sauk River. At present time, the North Fork originates in heavily logged terrain in the westside foothills, and its main stem forms a broad, flat valley that in recent years has seen extensive settlement. The North Fork's southside tributaries, notably Boulder Creek, drain rugged and wild alpine terrain with bold precipices such as Three Fingers and Whitehorse, drainages close to civilization but so dense with almost impassable vegetation as to be extremely remote if it were not for the few established trails.

The upper South Fork valley is certainly one of the most magnificent glacier valleys in the Cascades, even though it is cut off from the crest. The aftermath of the incredible excavating force of a river of ice can be seen in the north face of Big Four Mountain, a sliced and hacked wall of metamorphosed sedimentary rock that towers some 4,000 feet above the valley floor. This mountain is an especially spectacular sight in winter during the rare occasions when its snow-plastered face emerges from its usual shroud of dark, heavy clouds.

In its natural state, the upper South Fork was quite remote and inaccessible to native people and early explorers. Although the first major mining claims above the boomtown of Monte Cristo were discovered in 1889, Barlow Pass (near the headwaters of the the South Fork of the Stillaguamish), which turned out to be the key to Monte Cristo's major transportation route, was not discovered or recognized until the summer of 1891. In the same way that Stevens Pass eluded discovery, Barlow Pass, although it seems the obvious passageway today, took a surprising amount of time to find. Entry to Monte Cristo from the west was at first accomplished from the north by way of the Sauk River or from the south by way of the North Fork of the Skykomish. In the same way as other westside watersheds, the South Fork of the Stillaguamish in its natural state was thickly forested and choked with brush. The natives had made no profound changes to the landscape in this mountainous terrain, nor had they established any precedent of overland routes.

As soon as it was realized that Barlow Pass afforded by far the most direct (though not necessarily the easiest) route for shipping ore to the smelter at Everett, surveys for a railroad were conducted along the South Fork. Developers faced the dilemma of either building the railroad along the river, a route that necessitated an extensive tunnel system, or away from the river, a route that required long bridge spans. Unfortunately, they paid more attention to the immediate cost benefits of laying the rails along the river rather than considering how the South Fork could be transformed from a placid "trout stream" into a raging flood of destruction. Nevertheless, construction proceeded on no less than seven tunnels, as the rails followed the course of the river very closely. Even under the most stable of conditions, building the railroad was a dangerous enterprise. Due to an unstable slope of sand and mud, which collapsed during excavation, they had to abandon the idea of a seventh tunnel and reroute the line along a dubious curve. That first autumn, as the tunnels were being completed, a sample of what was to come occurred when the river rose above the rail line, flooding tunnels and knocking out bridges.

Despite the precarious nature of the enterprise, the railroad started operations in August of 1893. The seemingly Herculean task of transporting tons of ore, wrenched from deep within remote mountains that only years before had been hidden within a jungle of wilderness, was being accomplished. But what worked during benign summer weather would not necessarily work during the floods of the rainy season or the deep, heavy snows of winter. They overcame all the obstacles of running the line through the summer of 1897, but during that fall disaster struck. In November, after an ample early-season snowfall, warm rains deluged the area for days. Flood waters almost wiped out the entire rail line, smashed bridges, not only tore up the tracks but also tore up the landscape, leaving a horrible trail of debris. The damage was so severe that it looked like a deathblow for the railroad, but the mining fervor was not dead yet and the same line was rebuilt in 1900. From that time until the last gasp of organized effort in Monte Cristo in 1920, just about every fall and winter necessitated repeated efforts to repair damage from flooding, landslides, or avalanches.

Although summers are predictably dry, this watershed receives a tremendous amount of precipitation. As part of a convergence zone of moist flows of air that curl around the Olympic Mountains, its most moisture-prone areas usually receive something on the order of 180 or more inches per year. Sitka spruce and big-leaf maples with thick, clinging mats of moss grow near the base of Mt. Pilchuck, in a similar way as they grow in the Olympic rain forest. Species that do well in slightly drier climes just to the south, such as beargrass, do not grow here. In its natural state this area seldom burns, especially in the low elevation valleys, which stay soaked most of the year.

Only a small portion of the ancient trees that once grew in abundance up these deep valleys still remain. Past the dreary plots of even-aged trees and thickets, a trail to Heather Lake climbs through more monotonous second growth. Then, with suddenness as the trail rounds a bend, huge western red cedars soar into the sky. More such water-loving cedars cluster along this side of the valley growing very thick at the base digging their roots into the soaked inclines of Mt. Pilchuck. They make such sturdy foundations that they very seldom fall; although along streams they sometimes split, revealing the heartwood, intensely fragrant and a bright orange when wet. After a perpetual drenching, during which streams swell and crash down every ravine, the water still runs crystal-clear, filtered by a thick layer of humus laid down for centuries on the black slate bedrock.

Yellow monkey flowers, Goat Flats

Big Four Mountain, South Fork of the Stillaguamish Valley

Rime ice on alders and old growth, South Fork of the Stillaguamish 57

Snow-draped trees on the trail to Blanca Lake

Skykomish

THE ATTEMPT TO LINK THE NORTHERN PACIFIC RAILROAD with the West Coast in the second half of the 1800s motivated organized efforts to find a feasible pass north of Snoqualmie Pass. An exploration had some success in 1859 when E. F. Cady and another man hacked their way up the North Fork of the Skykomish and discovered an Indian route. Their way up the North Fork soon became a beaten path as miners and prospectors used it to develop claims along Silver Creek and then as an initial entryway to the Monte Cristo area. But despite the discovery of precious metals and promises of riches in the mountains, which certainly spurred the discovery of overland routes, Stevens Pass was not found until John Frank Stevens followed a highland approach along the Cascade Crest and looked down upon it for the first time in 1890.

From the west side it is not as if the Skykomish Valley is hidden from view. From a high point in Seattle or Everett one can see the obvious deep, glacial-carved trench and the steep-walled portals of the Cascade Range. More than anything, the time it took to discover Stevens Pass is testimony to how difficult it is to travel the deep, pathless valleys of the North Cascades. The engineer C. F. B. Haskell, who was charged with surveying the route for the railroad, wrote that there were no signs of trails within ten miles of either direction from the pass. It is known that the Skykomish Indians used the valley during the summers, but their impact was very slight, and they made few ventures overland. John Muir, who visited the Puget Sound area several years before the discovery of Stevens Pass, noted that the Indians saw little need for enterprise in the mountains and that their constructions were not even close to having the same effect on the land as beaver dams had.

Once the route over Stevens Pass was determined, construction of a railway began at a furious pace. The obstacles were formidable. Long bridge spans had to be constructed over six deep Skykomish Valley watercourses that crossed the intended route. In addition to the rugged terrain, engineers had to figure out how to deal with the steep incline up to the pass, especially steep on the west side. At first, before a tunnel could be constructed, precarious switchbacks were laid up the steep avalanche-prone hillsides. Obviously, at this point these entrepreneurs were not aware of the hazards of the terrain, of the deadly nature of the heavy winter snowpacks. Still, the railroad opened for service in 1893, and in what must have been an extraordinary stretch of good luck, it ran without major catastrophe until a tunnel could be completed in 1900.

Their struggle to build a tunnel was also fraught with danger. It took three long years for a large contingent of workers, suffering hard labor and severely trying work conditions, to bore 13,813 feet through the metamorphic rock of Stevens Pass. The workers had to contend with water pouring through loose shale intrusions and poor ventilation that resulted in unbearable temperatures and toxic fumes. The air quality became an even bigger problem once the line opened, as the locomotives pumped billows of smoke into the narrowed, confined space.

Even with a tunnel in place, these entrepreneurs had a great deal more to learn about the weather and terrain of this westside valley. They had constructed the tracks and tunnel without knowledge of the extended, seemingly endless snowstorms that can besiege the Cascades. On occasion, it will snow continuously; and even benign-looking slopes that otherwise never slide can avalanche in a horrendous way. It was during such an extended snowstorm in 1910 that a train full of people became trapped in what turned out to be a deadly spot. When slides overwhelmed the railroad's ability to clear the tracks, those marooned in railroad cars faced an impossible dilemma: either the hazard of staying put or what appeared to be the even greater hazard, walking out on foot through impossibly deep, heavy snow. Some were able to escape to the nearest outpost, climbing over the rock-hard avalanched mounds, swimming laboriously through the recent snow, and sliding blindly down a steep 800-foot slope. Those left behind watched in disbelief as the snow, which had been falling interminably, turned into a pouring rain. Then a huge slide, apparently triggered by shock waves from a lightening storm, pounded the valley. It was estimated at 2,000 feet wide and a half-mile long. About one hundred lives were lost as the two snowbound trains were swept off the tracks and buried beneath tons of avalanche debris.

An inquiry into the causes of the disaster absolved the railroad, basically laying the blame on Mother Nature. But pictures reveal that much of the dense forests that cloaked the steep hillsides had been reduced to stumps and stark, charred poles. Fires had occurred either out of intention in order to clear the land or by accident as in the case of random sparks flying from the steam locomotives. The bare slopes had undoubtedly altered the natural avalanche tracks and increased the potential and the extent of snow slides. Ordinarily, undisturbed North Cascades slopes have very definite avalanche tracks and trailings. The stability of local areas, especially in westside valleys, can be determined to some extent by the trees, which if left undeterred by slides or burns will grow thick and old.

Like other valleys in the North Cascades, the interior Skykomish Valley was worn down to its current depth mostly by glacial action and resultant pounding of meltwater. In some instances, the result of this grinding action of ice are spectacular faces such as the north wall of Bering Mountain and the north, east, and west walls of Mt. Index. These peaks do not rise to extraordinary elevations (Bering is only 6,125 feet and Mt. Index is even less than 6,000 feet), but they soar above a deep, extended valley floor (only 500 feet at the town of Index). In recent years the remaining glaciers, already shrunk to less than shadows of their former past, have been disappearing almost completely. In their wakes, there are now long water expanses in the gouged out granite bowls of the Foss and Miller drainages. Some of these lakes are very mundane now, easily approachable by well-trodden trails, but some are hidden beyond thick brush and granite, with long stretches of shimmering, wind-ruffled water disappearing into frequent mist and clouds.

Huckleberry and heather, Troublesome Mountain

Merchant Peak from Barcley Creek drainage

Douglas firs and western hemlock, West Cady Creek

Tank Lakes, Summit Chief, Chimney Rock, Middle Fork of the Snoqualmie Valley

Snoqualmie/Yakima

THE PROMINENT SNOQUALMIE PASS CORRIDOR is now a roaring conduit of vehicles through the Washington Cascades. It also provides a rough dividing line between the South Cascades, which are characterized by explosive volcanics and fluid flows of lava over wide spaces, and the North Cascades, which generally involve deep, precipitous valleys carved out of crystalline rock in various phases of metamorphism or of a granitic type. This dividing line is not always so straightforward, as the lowest pass over the Cascades requires a wide bend from both the Snoqualmie and Yakima River sides.

At a time before the frenetic traffic, when there were only faint Indian paths, Isaac Stevens, governor of the new and very wild Washington Territory, sought to determine a suitable railroad route through the Cascades to the growing centers of commerce on the Puget Sound. He enlisted Captain George McClellan with the formidable task of exploring unknown mountain territory of a very rugged and difficult kind. In the summer of 1853, McClellan could be found traveling north along the east side of the Cascades. It had not taken him very long to realize that the eastside open spaces were much less hampering to travel than the westside brush. After a very brief excursion to Lake Chelan, where he basically spent time rationalizing against making any substantial effort, in September he was exploring the wide-open upper valley of the Yakima River. The natives by this time had become suspicious of what McClellan's military venture was all about, and they were not very cooperative in providing guides or directions. Following the Yakima River to its source was an obvious choice for exploration. But McClellan, in the same way as subsequent travelers, was thrown off by the way the upper valley curves north to the lowest pass (Snoqualmie Pass) over the divide. He went straight west below Keechelus Lake and dropped down from the higher Yakima Pass to the west side. Gauging the amount of winter snow from the stains on the trees, noting the terrain, and not bothering to explore farther north, he concluded that even this area was unsuitable for a railroad pass.

Not willing to take no for an answer, Isaac Stevens called on Lieutenant Abiel Tinkham to show the feasibility of winter travel through the Snoqualmie Pass corridor. Tinkham was not unaccustomed to frightful winter travel, having only recently crossed from the Bitterroot Mountains to Fort Walla Walla. He knew how to travel efficiently under harsh and bitter conditions and also was able to establish a rapport with the natives. The snow level that particular January happened to be unusually low, certainly not indicative at all of the typical winter conditions. At the vicinity of Cle Elum Lake, at the last outpost, Tinkham dispensed with horses and even tents and set off on snowshoes with a group of Indians, relying on supplies of dried salmon and roots for sustenance. A bleak, colorless landscape with an uninspiring chill lay before them, but the going was good on the soft snow and across the long, frozen expanse of the lakes. Like McClellan, Tinkham missed the lowest, most feasible pass but had a relatively easy time crossing Yakima Pass and dropping into the Cedar River Valley. Luckily, he did not have to plunge through thick, heavy snow of great depth with the imminent threat of avalanches everywhere.

Today, many people flock to the lakes easily accessible from trailheads along the Snoqualmie Pass corridor. Starting next to the ragged fields of a ski area, the trail to Snow Lake, one of the most popular and accessible of Alpine Lakes destinations, climbs under mountain hemlocks, over moss-covered boulders and over frequent rills and boggy ravines. With any luck, the skies will remain misty and overcast, keeping the bugs at bay. From Snow Lake, the Rock Creek Trail descends into the deep, glacier-excavated Middle Fork of the Snoqualmie. Most people choose to access the Middle Fork using a logging road, a washout of glacial rubble, but to get the full flavor of the area a good exercise involves descending this ill-defined, no-longer-maintained trail for a several-thousand-foot vertical drop into the valley. After some easy switchbacks, the trail disappears into a tangle of salmonberry, huckleberry, ferns, and vine maple and hardly surfaces until some big, old trees are reached away from the prevalent avalanche tracks of the steep slope. Farther below is a beautiful moss-carpeted forest of Douglas firs and hemlocks, silent and still in the drifting fog. After a last obstacle of overgrown huckleberry thickets, the trail arrives at a converted logging road that parallels the Middle Fork on the valley bottom. On top of the glacial debris, stranded granite boulders, grows the thick vegetation of a long-standing, recycled coniferous forest, filtering and purifying the heavy precipitation that gushes and crashes down the channel of the Middle Fork.

To explore the drier east side, the modern adventurer can follow the early morning freeway flow past receding lights through the looming hills leading over Snoqualmie Pass. A good time to visit is autumn, just before the bite of winter tears away the final blazing colors of the landscape. On the east side the skies often clear, revealing bright, glinting stars past wisps of fog. After the turn for the North Fork of the Teanaway, the road continues to a dead end, at first over a smooth paved surface, then over a badly rutted washboard. At the start of the trail, the wind roars down the valley, tossing the treetops with fierce gusts, as clouds to the west vie with clearing to the east. In a crashing thud one tree falls to the ground. It's quite feasible here to leave the trail and travel cross-country, crossing the drainage lines over the frozen earth to the arm of Ingalls Peak. Snow starts falling as the light of dawn from the east grows brighter. The young trees grow thinner on the slope, giving way to an occasional whitebark pine or stunted subalpine fir and an open boulder slope of orange-encrusted serpentine rock. Once on top of the barren ridge of ice-glazed boulders, the wind blows fiercely cold, chasing away thoughts of rest. Above the frigid Ingalls basin, the veil of clouds begins to lift, revealing some of the snow-clad, black granite spires along the west ridge of Mt. Stuart.

Douglas fir and moss carpet, Middle Fork of the Snoqualmie Valley

Whiteback pines and serpentine rock, North Teanaway

Mt. Rainier, Emmons Glacier, the source of the White River

Mt. Rainier Watersheds

FROM ALL DIRECTIONS DEEP VALLEYS EXTEND to the base of Mt. Rainier at an elevation of not much more than 2,000 feet. The mountain itself rises to over 14,400 feet. With glaciers occupying on the order of 150 billion square feet, Mt. Rainier is obviously the center of dynamic watersheds radiating from an enormous bulk. The major rivers include the White, Carbon, Puyallup, Nisqually, and Cowlitz; all ultimately flowing west. None of them flow east to the Columbia.

An early expedition through the White River watershed over Naches Pass was led by Lieutenant Robert E. Johnson, who was a part of the United States Exploring Expedition (1838–1842) under Commander Charles Wilkes, an effort to gain more knowledge of Washington Territory. Several years later, the same route, or very nearly the same route, was traversed by Theodore Winthrop, whose name is commemorated by one of the spectacular glaciers on Rainier's north side. Whoever did the naming may have been playing a snide joke, for Winthrop scorned such nomenclature as he scorned the name of Rainier because natural wonders "should not be insulted by being named after indistinguished bipeds." He preferred the Indian word, "Tacoma," in the same way as he preferred Kulshan—"misnamed Mt. Baker by the vulgar," or the name of Whulge, "which uneducated maps call Puget Sound."

Winthrop's travels in the Cascades were certainly unique for such a time as 1853 in that they were self-initiated. This Don Quixote of Northwest explorers, Yale graduate, literary aficionado, sailed into Puget Sound and embarked on a basically solitary, overland journey going not west, along with the rising tide of pioneer emigration, but east, against the tide back to his native New England. This was at a time when the Northwest Indians were beginning to smolder at the behavior of the white man, who had become a serious threat to their way of life. His journey certainly was not for the faint of heart. He had several narrow escapes, not the least of which was a bout with smallpox, which may have aggravated his already frail health. The fruit of his expedition was a book called *Canoe and Saddle,* the most wonderful and outlandishly exuberant account ever written about the Cascades.

This most civilized of wilderness travelers, who could describe a meal of grouse cooked over an open fire as if he were the most discriminating epicure, left the Nisqually outpost for the wilds with a young Indian guide, three horses, and a little Northeastern snobbery. Although he was not without sympathy for his guide, he could not help seeing him as a conniving opportunist with slovenly habits. Loolowcan the Frowzy, he called him. Winthrop shared the same view as many of his contemporaries in the West, seeing the natives as children who had little focus in life, not much drive for making a better life for themselves. He was aware that the Indians were being boxed into a corner, and they were bound to react in ugly ways, especially when squeezed and humiliated. But he was completely exasperated with their dirty appearances, their unclean habits, their general lack of disciplined endeavor. Winthrop had business to attend to—he had to find a way through the Cascades and arrive at The Dalles in a set amount of time. This very timetable, along with being in alien territory, made him impatient and unwilling to tolerate loose action. But he was an explorer, a traveler, and he had no plans to contend with the natives for any of their resources or interfere with their way of life.

Throughout the journey he could not help but wince at the cruel treatment of the horses by the Indians, the pounding that his guide habitually gave to this most valued, living means of transport. His own attitude toward these essential trail companions wavered between exasperated amusement and sympathetic ministry. He relates his first impressions of one of the horses:

"a quadruped with the legs of an elephant, the head of a hippopotamus and a peculiar gait; - he trod most emphatically, as if he were striving to go through the world's crust at every step. This habit suggested the name he at once received. I called him Antipodes, in honor of the region he was aiming at, a name of ill omen, suggesting a spot where I often wished him afterwards.

This was at a time before extensive logging removed many of the tremendous forests that grew up the valleys leading to Mt. Rainier. The high overarching canopies and the thick trunks of giant trees extended for miles, only interrupted by scattered prairies and the river systems. They passed through ranks of Sitka spruces, with long, columnar mossy trunks and scaly purple bark, growing to great girths along the lower valley in a similar way as they still do in some spots in the Olympics today. On occasion these deep forests could appear like endless monotony, dark and foreboding, but they could also present an aspect of magic and wonder:

"It was an untenanted, silent forest, but silence here in this sunshiny morning I found not awful, hardly even solemn. Solitude became to me personal, and pregnant with possible emanations, as if I were a faithful pagan in those early days when gods were seen as men, and when under Grecian skies, Pan and the Naiads whispered their secrets to the lover of Nature."

They followed the course of the White River, fording the frigid, glacier-silted channel a number of times. Antipodes waywardly wondered into a deep pool, ruining their supply of hardtack. If anything, the undergrowth became more dense and entangling, and they had to fight with their horses to make progress. Despite the hard and lonesome traveling, Winthrop, with all the vigor of youth, could not help but be exuberant:

"Seediness of a morning is not the meed of him who has slept near Tacoma with naught but a green blanket and miles of elastic atmosphere between him and the stars. When I awoke, sleep fell from me suddenly, as a lowly disguise falls from a prince in a pantomime. I sprang up, myself, fresh, clear-eyed and with never a regretful yawn. Nothing was astir in nature save the river, rushing nigh at hand, and rousing me to my day's career by its tale of travel and urgency."

At this time there was an effort underway to complete a wagon route over the crest for the pioneers, to divert their numbers north into the Washington Territory. It was to be the first of many road-building efforts over hill and dale in this region. He describes how late one evening, his little group of wayfarers struggled in the darkening woods to see the blazes on the trees and to keep to the road, which had been recently cut. They could not find any grassy clearings that would provide forage for the wearied horses. At length, they came upon the campfire of a group of woodsmen who had been contracted to clear the road for the expected fall arrival of emigrants. What a sight Winthrop's straggly little contingent must have been to these workers: wanderers blundering in the dark, seeming to emerge almost out of nowhere into this wilderness. Winthrop assured them that he was not fleeing any crime, but making an innocent cross-country venture through the wilds of the Washington Territory.

Oftentimes the faint Indian path seemed preferable to the swath being cut in the forest, and Loolowcan followed it unerringly. With few prairies, the horses were suffering for food, and by the time they were required to struggle up the steep "ninety-degree" slope to the top of La Tete, they were in bad shape. As the little group dragged themselves above the forests, the astonishing gleaming bulk of Tacoma rose along with them.

Especially from the north and northeast Rainier is a sight to behold! By the late summer, last season's excess winter snow has melted off the sheer, north-facing Willis Wall, revealing part of the treacherous bare rock, the precarious ice of the summit glacier and the huge ice amphitheater created by the Carbon Glacier. On the northeast side, the Emmons, the largest of Rainier's glaciers, and the Winthrop Glacier extend as long cracked and fissured slopes from the summit into the upper reaches of the White River watershed. During the summer months there is no question as to the how the White River was named—it is loaded with glacial sediment and approaches the turbidity of skimmed milk. Old trees line this waterway throughout the public lands portion of its flow, but such stability has not always been the case nor is it promised. Underneath its placid and reigning exterior, Rainier is a simmering caldron that continually vents hot gases from the fiery depths of the earth. Considering the softness of the volcanic rock and something like 150 billion square feet of glacier, pressure building within the earth is a sign of disaster. Indeed, as recently as about 5,600 years ago, an explosion of the summit and subsequent melt of the Emmons Glacier caused an onslaught of mud to charge down this valley, reaching as far as the Puget Sound, inundating the plain where the thriving towns of Enumclaw, Puyallup, Auburn, and even Kent are currently located.

Only a few years after Theodore Winthrop left the Northwest, a military man named August Valentine Kautz viewed the imposing presence of Mt. Rainier from his post at Fort Steilacom long enough and with enough youthful longing to want to climb it. Though Kautz writes that he had a "passion for going to the tops of high places," the likelihood is that he had no alpine experience, as he describes preparations based on reading books about ascents of glaciated peaks such as Mt. Blanc. But after talking about the undertaking long enough, he had no choice but to make the attempt. His friends, who had been quite eager to go, had second thoughts when they saw that he was actually serious.

At that time, quite possibly someone had climbed Rainier, but Kautz knew of no accounts nor of any European who had been anywhere close to the mountain. He learned from the Indians that the Nisqually was the most approachable (if it could be called approachable) river valley, and he managed to procure an old Indian guide named Wah-pow-e-ty. Kautz relates that almost from the start, just ten or twelve miles out of Steilacom, they entered an immense, virtually untouched evergreen forest that sprawled out along the Cascade Range. The trail at that time ended at the Mishal prairie, one of only a few isolated prairies, lone interruptions to the vast tract of trees.

Considering that he was commencing the trailless part of his journey west of the present-day town of LaGrande, the six days he allotted for the trip seem laughable. In fact, it took the group almost that amount of time just to emerge from the dense forest onto the base of the Nisqually Glacier. The natives at one time or another had ventured up the Nisqually, but for Kautz and his three other companions (referred to as Carrol, Dogue, and the doctor), it was as if they had to cut through an almost impenetrable wilderness. There was no easy way. They had the choice of either seeking the heights of the adjoining hills over jumbles of fallen logs and up-and-down terrain, or the tangles and thickets along the muddy torrent that roared down the eroded river channel. The way was not made any easier by foolish inexperience, as in the case of the doctor, who chose to fill his canteen with whisky (the most readily available painkiller) on the first day. As they persisted in hacking their way farther upstream into what is now Mt. Rainier National Park, the skies, which earlier had been clear and offered at least a few cheerful views, turned gloomy and foreboding. They camped along what is now called Kautz Creek, not far from today's thoroughfare of summertime visitors. It was an eerie, threatening place then:

> *"The gloomy forest, the wild mountain scenery, the roaring of the river, and the dark overhanging clouds, with the peculiar melancholy sighing which the wind makes through a fir forest, gave to our camp at this point an awful grandeur"*
> *"Night set in with the drizzling rain, and a more solitary, gloomy picture than we presented at that camp it is impossible to conceive ... the solitude was oppressive"*

As the gorge narrowed and became more precipitous, they fought their way more slowly, sensing the concussive action of avalanches and the roaring river. In a cold rain they climbed onto the mud-stained ice of the main Nisqually glacier, and then in a driving sleet storm wound their way past the yawning blue gashes of ice and struggled up a crumbling, near vertical moraine to the last of the straggly trees, where they made camp. It was a strange environment for them. They spent some time wondering if the splayed hoof prints in the soft soil had anything to do with the burrows in the ground, realizing that the prints were made by a large mammal (mountain goat) but not realizing that they had nothing to do with marmot homes.

As they got started next morning, it was not long before Kautz realized that the summit was much farther from camp than the three hours he envisioned. They caught glimpses of the glaciated rock above, and soon made enough progress to break above the clouds, viewing an ocean of clouds and the glacial islands of Mt. Hood, Adams, and St. Helens spread out before them. Gradually, those low clouds dispersed, and they must have felt for a time that the place was not nearly as menacing as it was spectacular. But the going was unrelenting, and they had little familiarity with the effects of the thin air at such a high elevation, nor had they anticipated the burning and blinding sun as it reflected mercilessly off the snow. Kautz relates that late in the afternoon he had outdistanced all his companions and reached a point where the mountain leveled off onto the summit ridge. But a hostile, frigid wind had blown his cap away, an icy crust was forming on what had been mushy snow, and the water inside his canteen had begun to freeze. Seeing no alternative but to freeze to death, he joined his exhausted companions, and succeeded in getting down the mountain and safely to camp, despite one of his companions sliding out of control for forty or so feet.

Thirteen years later, the way up the Nisqually had changed very little, although there was by then a dim trail for some distance beyond Mishall prairie. In August of 1870, Hazard Stevens, Philo Van Trump, and Edmund Coleman (the same Coleman who first climbed Mt. Baker) faced the same kind of arduous enterprise as Kautz. James Longmire, an early settler along the Nisqually who later discovered Longmire Hot Springs and made an ascent of Rainier, guided them through the initial stretch and helped them procure a native guide named Sluiskin. Coleman proved not up to the task mainly because of age and a recent illness, but he did provide essential equipment to Stevens and Van Trump.

Sluiskin turned out to be an interesting character, one for whom Stevens showed a high regard. A Native American, he lived most of his life in the wilderness, enduring the hard lessons of always dealing directly with the elements, living with a strong sense of independence. Despite his isolation within the thickets of the Nisqually and Cowlitz, he had managed to learn the Chinook Jargon as well as a notable amount of English and he was shrewd and keen in his expression. Sluiskin led them over a high route along the Tatoosh Range, one he was familiar with owing to his wanderings hunting mountain goats. They passed over the marvelous flower meadows (now called Paradise Meadows) and past clumps of the arrowlike spires of subalpine firs to a camp somewhere on Mazama Ridge. It was at their campfire in the wild night, according to Stevens, that Sluiskin delivered a long warning against attempting to reach the summit of Rainier. Stevens later remembered the Chinook language that Sluiskin used and translated it in detail. How Sluiskin's grandfather had attempted the ascent but had come upon a "fiery lake" and an "infernal demon coming to destroy him." How the initial joy of climbing over the snowfields becomes peril as rocks come hurdling down and the surface becomes slippery enough that any misstep is enough to send one plunging into an abyss. How there are immense and deep crevasses to circumvent. How, if the climber is lucky enough to reach the summit ridge, he then must encounter a biting and hostile wind that will most likely blow him away; and if, by some miracle he is still alive despite the cold, then the "mighty demon of Tahkoma" will surely throw him into a "fiery lake."

The next day Stevens and Van Trump showed no signs of shrinking from Sluiskin's dire warnings as they pushed high up the mountain, progressing past projectiles of falling rocks, cutting steps in the treacherous ice, and winding their way around crevasses to the fierce wind of the barren summit ridge, to the same point that Kautz had reached. They even showed a reckless abandon by not taking either coats or blankets, or enough food and water, and a lot less discretion than Kautz by proceeding ahead to Point Success, where they staged a celebration. The wonder of it was that they were able to astonish Sluiskin by returning. Instead of a "mighty demon," a guardian angel must have assisted them in surviving bitter and savage conditions. Luckily, they managed to locate fumeroles of hot gases and an ice cave, allowing them to spend a thoroughly miserable night but to come out alive. By miraculously returning, ever since, they have been honored as the first to reach the summit of Rainier.

Since Stevens and Van Trump, many have been spared the illusion of accomplishment by not reaching the summit and experiencing Rainier as a force of nature. In 1894 steam and black smoke of what turned out to be a minor eruption, the only eruption of Rainier in recorded history, was observed from populated areas around Puget Sound. There was enough curiosity that a Seattle newspaper sponsored a winter expedition in order to determine what could not be seen behind the winter blanket of clouds. Edward S. Ingraham was chosen to lead a group of five up the Carbon River Valley with the intention of crossing the north side of the mountain and climbing the Emmons Glacier. Ingraham knew something about Mt. Rainier, having climbed it at least once in the summer. But Rainier is a very different place in December, and they were ill prepared for the inevitable obstacles of such a long and hard journey. All they had for braving the arctic conditions were several layers of woolen clothes. The entire expedition was a test of their resolve, with the exception of an unseasonably warm first day and a few comfortable moments at camp.

The journey began at Wilkeson, which was then an outpost of a few miners and stragglers, several days travel from what is now the national park, along the obstacle course of the Carbon River. On the second day, having reached the end of the trail, they were forced to do twenty-three crossings of the frigid river while following the course of the channel. Soaked and bedraggled as darkness set in, they searched for a dry campsite, giving up on finding enough dry wood for a fire. They proceeded up the valley into progressively deeper snow to the base of the Carbon Glacier, where in the morning they were surprised by the sudden clearing and a view of the spectacular north side of the mountain. But such a sight as the immense glaciated face glistening out of the blue lasted only briefly as it began to storm. From this place onward, they were at the mercy of the elements, never able to get any protracted rest without feeling the biting cold, having to cut their way for a time through a blizzard. That night they struggled hard to find a sheltered nook among the tough, surviving conifers, feeling vulnerable and alone, finding kinship in the howling of a lone timber wolf in between the booms and crashes of avalanches from above.

They did have a link with the outside world: carrier pigeons, which they periodically released along the way. On Christmas Eve day, as they passed through the arctic wasteland of what in summer are almost truly the "Elysian fields," the skies cleared, allowing them a view of the summit, where for the first time they could glimpse the unusual plumes of steam and smoke, which by this time must have seemed like just another aspect of an awesome natural spectacle. Several warm springs in the otherwise frozen surface were a relief to their thirst but made them wonder how much they could count on solid footing. That night, after viewing a sunset splashed with every sort of color, they huddled together and shivered through the blasting wind without sleep the entire night, looking out over the wild star-filled sky. On Christmas Day they carefully crossed through the gashes of the Winthrop Glacier to Steamboat Prow, and realized, as they saw the snow clouds surrounding them, that they could not endure the harsher realm above them.

The Carbon Glacier, Liberty Ridge, North Face of Mt. Rainier

The retreating Nisqually Glacier

Cedar and Douglas firs, White River Valley

Subalpine firs and silver firs, Naches Peak

Lupines, wallflower, typical volcanic rock of the east side

Naches/Tieton

CONTINUING "THE STORY OF A CIVILIZED MAN'S SOLITARY ONSLAUGHT AT BARBARISM," Theodore Winthrop crossed the Cascade Divide at Naches Pass on his way to the Columbia River at The Dalles. He and his (not exactly faithful) guide Loolowcan dropped into the narrow gorge of the Naches River, "the via mala," leaving behind the lushly vegetated, temperate west side for the desiccated scarps and blazing sun of the eastern basins, not to mention the disgruntled natives.

They did not have to go far before they ran into Captain George McClellan and his cohorts. According to Winthrop they were poking their heads into the eastside valleys and canyons in search of a route for the Northern Pacific Railroad. Captain McClellan, in the same way as his explorations to the north, was not having much success in finding passes through the mountains. As the country of the lower Naches opened, the sun became more blazing and wearisome, and Winthrop's little group entered the summer grounds of the nomadic Klickitat tribe. They were accosted here by one of Loolowcan's tribe members, whom Winthrop could not help comparing unfavorably to the "seediest ragamuffin" he had ever seen. At their next stop, the Klickitat encampment (Winthrop called it Stenchville), his unease concerning their dreary and even putrid conditions may have added insult to injury and aroused the inhabitants into what could have been a deadly encounter. Winthrop was forced to strike out on his own with his three straggly horses over rolling, sagebrush plains where he could not quite get the direction correct. From that point, he would have been lost, easy prey for any plundering vagrant or highway robber, were it not for his good fortune of finding an excellent Indian guide, who guided him the final eighty miles through a terrific storm to the Dalles.

The Naches River, which these early explorers followed, flows into the Yakima River, and every year the snowpack of the Cascades provides irrigation water to the farmlands and fruit orchards of the Yakima Valley. The source of this life-providing resource has not always gone unnoticed, as for example, at the turn of the twentieth century, when valley ranchers complained bitterly about sheepherders who radically altered the landscape of the higher hills in order to provide summer pasture for their flocks. Burning the ridges and then turning the sheep loose to chew the grasses down to the roots destroyed the vegetation that had been largely responsible for extending the lingering snowpack over part of the summer months and moderating the spring runoff.

Not only are the Cascades the source of life-giving water to places such as Yakima, but they have been a source of inspiration as well, as in the case of William O. Douglas, former justice of the Supreme Court. Douglas spent his youth in Yakima; and when he could, he roamed the highlands north of Adams and east of Mt. Rainier, drawing the power of inspiration that these mountains are known to impart to its admirers. During his childhood he was afflicted by infantile paralysis, and he found that taking long rambles in the mountains was a way to gain strength and confidence.

Douglas was a twentieth-century man, not an early explorer, but many of his writings evoke those days of mystery before signposts or maps, when the natives revered the mountains as abodes of spirits.

"When I left the road at Soda Springs, I was at once in a deep forest that no axe had ever touched. Great yellow pine [ponderosa pine] reached to the sky, one hundred, two hundred feet. This was the dry, eastern slope of the Cascades. There was little underbrush; the woods were open, not dense. The sun came streaming in, as if it were pouring through long narrow windows high in a cathedrel. The soft notes of some bird—a thrush, I believe—came floating down from the treetops. As I listened it was as though the music came from another world."

He writes of befriending a Yakima Indian who was spearing salmon along the Tieton River, using the same method as Lewis and Clark described. Giant, battered salmon up to fifty pounds relentlessly made their way against the crashing rapids of the Columbia and its tributaries on the way to their spawning grounds hundreds of miles from the ocean. Douglas recounts seeing them high in eastside streams of the Cascades, streams narrow enough to be jumped.

Indian legends and stories reveal the need to explain the mysterious forces of nature and creation, which are forever changing the landscape, presenting to the inhabitants great wonders. A mysterious force drove the salmon in their fattened condition from the Pacific Ocean into the pounding streams, through a long, foodless obstacle course to the beds of their birthplaces, their final destination where they spawned a new generation and then died. Their bounty did not always occur, and in those years the natives suffered famine. When the walls bounding the Columbia collapsed and blocked the river, creating the Bridge of the Gods, the salmon may have been blocked from making their usual migrations to the east side.

The natives chose to deify the coyote because they had observed that in a hostile and changeable world, the coyote had the tenacity and cunning to survive, even though the coyote was relatively small and weak. The coyote was the trickster, the character in a mythic interpretation who decided a natural catastrophe or event, as if symbolizing a spirit that actualized events. When the settlers arrived, they considered the coyote a nuisance and did everything they could to eradicate its presence from the land with any weapon they could use. All to no avail.

As the blazing summer sun sears the eastside slopes, the dust thickens on the trails and the lush flowers wilt and turn to seed. The wearied trail traveler finds faint comfort in the listless calls of birds or in the still, heated shadows, while getting constantly harassed by deer flies, inspired by the languid hot weather into a relentless stinging of flesh. But the huckleberries have ripened, luscious fruit from the long, mountain days of brilliant sunshine. Since all the snowbanks have long since melted, obtaining water requires dropping into one of basins to reach a trickling spring.

If there is no threat of evening lightning storms, a good place to make camp, once some water can be obtained, is on top of the crumbling volcanic ruins of an old fire lookout such as Noble Knob. At one time a whole section of the ridge was racked by a lightning-caused fire. Over the open meadows, overripe and going to seed, stand the single ghostly, sun-bleached snags, their limbs busted, sole upright relics of the bygone hearty subalpine firs so resistant to the battering winds, bitter cold, or harsh sunlight. Many such limbs have fallen and lie quietly rotting into the ground at odd and grotesque angles.

The evening draws slowly on, with the sun losing it blaze as it draws closer to the haze and forest fire smoke hung along the horizon. Soon, the sun turns into a vermilion ball and then loses all flicker and shine as it slips out of sight into the grayness. The stars start appearing faintly and the sense of loneliness in this wild place is eased as the land suspires, soothed by the breezes from the west. One feels much freer to take on the inactivity, the unhurried state, like being on an island, cast off from the impulse of having to get something done.

In the dark, early morning with the air freshened, the old quarter moon shining intensely and the stars brilliant flecks of light, below in a ravine a coyote lets loose with loud prolonged cries: a wild screaming and wailing subsiding into a yapping and going on and on, echoing against the rock cliffs. It could be a cry of a renegade just wailing loud and long, or a wild and adolescent cry of bravado, or not to be discounted: a cry of defiance from an animal that has been persecuted and hated in any number of ways beyond its control and beyond any reason but has the wits to survive and at this unknown, beautiful time of night can flourish and celebrate the spirit of the land.

Subalpine firs and paintbrush, Norse Peak

Whitebark pine snags, Naches ridges

Mt. St. Helens, pre-1980 eruption

Mt. St. Helens and Mt. Adams Watersheds

"Dearest charmer of all is St. Helens, queen of the Cascades, queen of North America, a fair and graceful volcanic cone. Exquisite mantling snow sweep along her shoulders toward the bristling pines. Sometimes she showers her realms with a boon of light ashes, to notify them that her peace is repose, not stupor, and sometimes lifts a beacon of tremulous flame by night from her summit." — THEODORE WINTHROP

IN A FLURRY OF ACTIVITY FROM MARCH TO MAY OF 1980, Mt. St. Helens transformed itself from the "fair and graceful" mountain with a beautiful glaciated mantle to a blown-out shell with a long trail of mud and dust. Spirit Lake, which had been a blue jewel set below an emerald forest of silver firs, subalpine firs, and mountain hemlocks, turned into a thick, gray soup of sediments clotted with logs. The hills of Mt. Margaret, once vibrant with green meadows and brilliant flower displays, changed into barren, dust fields of gray ash and blasted trees.

It has been noted that this most recent violent episode was just another transformation of the volcano's form. In the Indian myth of the "Bridge of the Gods" Loowit, an ugly witch, was transformed into a lovely maiden, perhaps reflecting its actual change after frequent eruptions some 400–500 years ago. The myth involved a love triangle concerning the beautiful Loowit and two jealous admirers, Klickitat and Wy'east, the original names of Mt. Adams and Mt. Hood.

As in other Northwest places, the bogus promise of mineral wealth motivated interest in the St. Helens area. Nineteenth-century explorers of the North Fork of the Lewis River brought back a few specks of gold that they had somehow managed to extract from the sandbars along the crystal-clear watercourses. Word of these meager discoveries spread and suggested that there was a vast wealth there for the finding. The fortune seekers who fell for this exaggeration had to settle for less materialistic pursuits, for the astonishing natural beauty of Mt. St. Helens rising above huge Douglas firs and crystalline streams. Such worthless but inspiring pursuits as climbing to its summit in those days was a considerably greater enterprise than today. Unless the explorers followed a beaten track, such as George McClellan's path in 1853, they depended on direction from the Indians, who kept warning them of evil spirits that prowl the mountaintop.

St. Helens has never been a particularly difficult peak to climb, but it has acquired a mystique, and to the Indians of the nineteenth century it was an object of awe and fear. The settlers at Vancouver and along the Columbia had noticed a series of eruptions from 1831–1857 that sent smoke and steam into the atmosphere and darkened its snowy mantle. The mountain spewing fire, as well as some unusual lava rock formations, which have invited an image of a weird, hirsute, primitive, ape-like creature called a sasquatch, have lent a sense of lore and mystery to the area, which those making the first ascent must have felt.

St. Helens and its companion Mt. Adams are situated nearly on the same latitude and are separated by almost thirty-five air miles. Between them extends a highland divide, called the Dark Divide, that forms an unusual watershed boundary between north and south. All the drainage to the north flows into the Cispis River and all the drainage to the south flows into the Lewis River. In its natural state, the area is heavily forested, with the exception of high points such as Shark Rock and Craggy Peak and where the terrain has been racked by fire and the recent eruption of Mt. St. Helens. Numerous streams of clear mountain water originate from this highland divide. Of special note are Quartz and Clear Creeks, which originate and flow through heavily forested areas to the south, and McCoy and Yellowjacket Creeks, which divide fire-cleared ridges to the north.

Especially prominent in the deep woods are the columnar trunks of the old Douglas firs. They are not everywhere and in some places, such as along the Lewis River, they have been burned out and are now decaying shells. They stand on their own mounds that they build by shedding bark, twigs, and lichens. Their deep, furrowed bark gives them a solemn aspect, a quality of age, an indication of having withstood the vicissitudes of weather and much longer times than human beings. As they grow older, they become more distinctive, often broken at the top or scarred by bygone summer fires, with sprawling shaggy branches festooned with lichen and growing far above the ground. As they tower over the quiet forest floor, bold enough to grow several hundred feet tall, they impart a venerable air to their surroundings.

A deep layer of pumice from the explosive St. Helens covers most of the ground of the Dark Divide. The undergrowth is sparser toward the east and quite amenable to elk, whose herds cut deep trails into the soft soil of the steep hillsides. Although the pumice soil is quite porous and generally prevents the formation of wetlands and lush summer flower meadows, tree growth is hardly deterred. Yellowjacket Creek provides some of the best conditions for noble fir anywhere; the largest known noble fir, as well as others of significant size and beauty, grows in this valley.

A lot less active volcano in recent times is Mt. Adams, a majestic glaciated dome rising high above an ancient spill of basalt. Considering the millions of years spanning the geological life of the Cascades, Adams is a mere youth. As in the Oregon Cascades and as far north of Snoqualmie Pass, the crest here was once overspread by fluid flows of lava. The approach to Adams is relatively gradual, through the arrowy spires of subalpine firs, strongly scented and in summer shading wood rushes and forming glades amidst profuse meadows of blue and lavender lupines. Closer to the mountain the firs and flowers become more stunted, enduring icy blasts of wind and the meager growing season.

Mt. St. Helens, post-1980 eruption

Noble fir and vine maple, Upper Yellowjacket Valley

Lewis River during autumn

View of Mt. Rainer from The Dark Divide

SECTION II divides the Oregon Cascades into the most prominant watersheds—those areas of land that drain into the major river systems that either flow into the Columbia River or directly into the Pacific Ocean.

Map of the Oregon Cascades Watersheds

Oregon oak and Metlako Falls, Eagle Creek (Spring)

Columbia River Gorge

"The scenery at this season is likewise grand beyond description; the high mountains in the neighborhood, which are for the most part covered with pines of several species, some of which grow to an enormous size, are all loaded with snow; the rainbow from the vapour of the agitated water, which rushes with furious rapidity over shattered rocks and through deep caverns producing an agreeable although at the same time a somewhat melancholy echo through the thick wooded valley; the reflections from the snow on the mountains, together with the vivid green of the gigantic pines, form a contrast of rural grandeur that can scarcely be surpassed."
— DAVID DOUGLAS

THE COLUMBIA RIVER FORMS A BREACH in the Cascade Mountains where the water draining such faraway places as Jackson Hole and the Canadian Rockies has sliced a channel on its imperious way to the Pacific. Though the landforms of Washington and Oregon have changed drastically in the last thirty million years or so, the Columbia has continued to find a way to the Pacific. Even during the lava floods that spread as far as Idaho to the channel of the Columbia, the river has continued to cut a path.

Part of a long history of cataclysmic events, the most recent occurred toward the end of the last Ice Age advance, when as a result of the melting of the immense Cordilleran ice sheet, floods of water poured through the Gorge on the way to the Willamette Valley. Water and rock debris pounded the channel with a tremendous erosional force that scoured out the banks up to something like a thousand vertical feet and broadened the valley.

When the pioneers finally arrived at The Dalles, on the verge of the promised land after the hardships of the Oregon Trail, they had to contend with one last formidable obstacle. After the long stretches of arid, dust clouded wasteland, where they plodded along with their oxen teams it-seemed-like-forever under a harsh, brutal sun against an ever-receding horizon; they now faced the hurdle of crossing the wet, thickly vegetated Cascades just as the rainy season commenced.

At that time, the Columbia River, which splits the Cascades as the lowest elevation pass in Washington or Oregon (not much higher than sea level), had a wild character. Though not interrupted by severe waterfalls west of The Dalles, it offered a formidable obstacle of rapids lined with rocks and thick vegetation, which at least on occasion could be a nightmare for the wearied travelers, many of whom were on their last legs. Until an enterprising pioneer named Samual Barlow cut a wagon trail across the Cascades just south of Mt. Hood, the transportation difficulties of the Columbia Gorge were the only option. Typically, the emigrants would arrive late in the fall and would have to contend with the dark, dismal rains that would descend upon them from the never-ending march of clouds from the west.

Like with many of the emigrants who would come later, Lewis and Clark arrived late in the season, just in time for the onset of the November rains. On a cold, rainy day they approached the narrowing moss-covered walls through which the wild river crashed over a wreckage of rock. In their journals they wrote about the "Great Shute," the narrow channel that extended a half a mile. They followed the Indians who portaged their canoes over treacherous rocks and then two and a half miles more to avoid a second "shute." The mountain range subsequently received its name from these cascades that occurred as a result of huge rockslides from the adjoining basalt rock formations. The slides appear to have occurred around eight hundred years ago and, for a time, actually blocked the river, inspiring the native peoples to call the blockage the Bridge of the Gods. Immense and incomprehensible forces were at work, which for a time may have blocked their vital food supply, the abundant annual migrations of salmon from the sea.

When Lewis and Clark ventured up the Columbia, they were astonished at the number of salmon both dead and alive along the shore and deep within the exceptionally clear water. The natives largely subsisted on the bounty of these ocean-running fish, as well as roots and berries, and showed little ambition for technological advancement. They had no use for agriculture, viewing such labors as a needless intrusion upon the sacredness of Mother Earth. With their immediate needs well provided for, they lived a dreamlike existence, not prodded by the struggles of hard work. It was a stress-free kind of life, but those considering such a life a paradise would have needed a certain tolerance for the cold, damp drafts of winter, fleas everywhere in summer, and a confusion of grime and strange aromas from many people sharing the same rough shelter built from crude wood planks. Everywhere else in the Cascades, the natives lived as nomads, not regarding the land as anyone's possession; but along the Columbia they had established domestic permanence, based in large part on fishing rights.

By the time of Lewis and Clark, the heyday of these people had already seen a decline due to a relentless tide of disease that had found its way inland from the coast, arriving there with the European explorers. But their populations were still significant along the river, especially during the summer season when the salmon runs and central locality drew many clustering along the shores. The crowds from the villages proved a gauntlet for Alexander Ross when he made excursions into the interior from a base in Astoria along the coast. Despite the fact that the fur traders were interested mainly in trading with the natives and were in no serious competition, weapons were usually within easy reach and there was no power of law. Combined with the lawless plundering of at least some of the early traders was a natural possessiveness on the part of the natives concerning the Columbia and its resources. But despite murders, which occurred on both sides as the result of disputes, an uneasy truce usually prevailed.

But worse than any bloody battle during those languid river days was another wave of disease, probably malaria and smallpox. In their dreams the natives must have looked upon the increasing appearance of the white explorers and then settlers as some strange alien invasion as if from another planet, menacing and insidious when entire villages suddenly grew sick and most died.

Several decades later, in his second westward expedition of 1843–44, John Charles Fremont passed through the Columbia River Gorge on his way back and forth from Ft. Vancouver for supplies. The numerous Indian villages were by this time largely gone, but the wild scenery had changed hardly at all, although Fremont makes no mention of wildlife such as seals that Lewis and Clark had reported as quite common (although they mistakenly called them sea otters). On the passage west, Fremont's group was blessed with idyllic weather and enjoyed a respite from their intense journeying in feasts of salmon. At first, traveling by night under the beacon of the moon, they were born west in their canoes by the strong easterly wind gusts of the Gorge under the dark, looming basalt walls. The next morning, under a rare November sun, they approached the cascades, which occurred after a short turn south where the river broke over "agglomerated masses of rock."

Here, they beached the canoes and, as had become the custom, sought the assistance of the Indians in making the portage. Fremont also observed the "submerged forest," the dead trees visible underneath the "beautifully clear water," which he speculated were due to massive landslides that blocked the river and diverted the channel. After resuming their water journey on the lower rapids, they passed the vertical cliffs with their marvelous waterfalls, most notably Multnomah Falls. On their way back, they were not so fortunate in the weather. They had to fight against formidable east winds that were so violent that one day they could make no progress. When the pouring rain extinguished their evening campfires, everyone spent a miserable night, with the possible exception of the seasoned voyageurs, who, of course, never complained.

Today, big trucks roar along the interstate highway linking east and west along the Columbia River. The commerce has become all the more bustling and frenetic, eclipsing the old days when it was an attainment just to arrive in the Willamette Valley. With the exception of trails, the magnificent steep-walled canyons on the Oregon side of the Gorge have changed hardly at all in several hundred years. The dark basalt, residue of massive volcanic flows long before the Pleistocene Ice Age, is almost always covered with thick carpets of vivid green moss and duff except under overhanging walls and along rushing watercourses.

After the ice storms, floods, or snow of winter have stilled the life in the canyons, the place comes alive in the spring, particularly in April. The soft spring rain and warming temperatures bring to life a delicate, lush ground cover, lilies and larkspur on the open slopes, vivid shades of green from the buds and blooms of the big-leaf maples. The pounding runoff roars through narrow slots such as Oneata Gorge and Eagle Creek and sprays and gushes over the moss-clad cliffs.

Moss wall above Tanner Creek

Waterfall along Oneata Creek

Oregon oak and Metlako Falls, Eagle Creek (Winter)

Mt. Hood from the Muddy Fork of the Sandy River

Mt. Hood Watersheds

AFTER THE SUMMER SUN HAS BLAZED AWAY INTO EARLY AUTUMN, Mt. Hood looks more like what it really is—a large pile of volcanic debris. But catch a view of it on one of those rare, clear winter days after the long onslaught of blizzards above tree level. Its serrated ridges are plastered with shimmering snow, shadowed by the diminished winter light, merged into a spire set against the deep blue of the frigid sky, rising more than a mile above any other high point in the area.

In the long advance of geological time, Mt. Hood is merely one more eruption of volcanic rock, which over time will be worn away as its predecessor was worn away. As the highest point in the Oregon Cascades, it stands now as an imposing solitary presence, a lone barrier against especially fierce storms that batter its summit with ice. It impressed the earliest of explorers, and the emigrants, especially when they first caught a glimpse of its snow sentinel after months of slogging over the scorched plains.

The Forest Service had the audacity to place a fire lookout on the summit in 1915. Certainly, if it should chance to be clear, the summit's commanding position is a perfect site for fire observation: the rolling forest lands of the Clackamas watershed, the Bull Run watershed forests, the Sandy River forests to the west, and the Hood River forests to the east. Only a person with a deep love of the mountains, such as Elijah Coalman, could have maintained a lookout in such a setting; only one who could say with utmost conviction as he did, "a sunrise or sunset from the top of a mountain is a treat of a lifetime." To climb the slopes of Mt. Hood is to leave behind the easy, reliable comforts for the uncertainties of a lonely, snowy wasteland reaching into the sky. One time, he and a companion spent several days clinging to their lives as incredible gale-force winds threatened to blow them into the Eliot Glacier below the north face. When the sun finally emerged through the thick, driving mist and they could see more than a foot ahead, everything in sight was coated with glaring ice, in places several feet thick. Besides the dangerous storms, merely reaching the top, let alone ferrying supplies or building materials, could be an ordeal. In August a menacing crevasse opened just below the summit ridge, and a rickety ladder was used to cross it. Coalman learned to navigate with unbelievable speed up and down the often fogbound, spooky ice and snow, and would appear as a godsend to rescue wayward and stricken climbers. But Coalman paid for his exploits, generous though they were, as he suffered serious injury from being pounded in the chest by a rock. The man who had lived for rarefied, physical adventure amongst the severe and beautiful mountain elements had to learn to live a more confined life.

Mt. Hood appears to have developed relatively late in the long period of glaciation, the Pleistecene Epoch. Before the last major glacial advance, it had attained its full stature of some 12,000 feet in elevation and was probably as symmetrical as Mt. St. Helens before the 1980 eruption. Glaciers severely eroded its symmetry, tearing away its central vent from the constant gnawing of ice on the north side. The present-day south-facing crater that steams and reeks of sulfur developed from a side vent. Like other stratovolcanos of advanced age and size, the molten rock within its core has become very high in silica, making it very viscous and increasing the chances of explosive eruptions. The most recent eruptions occurred about 1790–1810, sending mudflows down the White, Sandy, and Zigzag Rivers, along areas that now have become increasingly developed and populated. When Lewis and Clark traveled the Columbia River in 1805–06, they noted that the mouth of the Sandy River was clogged by mud and debris, a condition no longer apparent today.

The valleys surrounding Mt. Hood nurture dense coniferous forests, making Samuel Barlow's efforts in 1845 to navigate and then to build a toll road around the south side of Mt. Hood an arduous enterprise. But Barlow was a man of determination and action. Stranded at The Dalles waiting interminably for a flimsy boat to ferry his group at an exorbitant price down the final stretch to the Willamette Valley, he resolved to fight his way through the Cascades. The old, experienced mountain men and anyone else acquainted with the territory thought he was out of his mind. After all, it was already late September, and they and their stock had already made the long trek across the western frontier. Barlow may never have imagined the ordeal that awaited him in attempting to convey a group of pioneer families with their precious possessions across the Cascades as winter approached. At first, the going was relatively easy across arid, rolling hills of Oregon oak and yellow pine. The hard work of lowering and then raising the wagonloads from the chasm of Tygh Creek was by that time more routine than a hardship, as was the drop down to the glacial runoff of the White River. But once they confronted the dense forests and swamps toward Barlow Pass and Summit Meadows, their progress was seriously impeded. The only food that was readily available off the land was huckleberries. Without anything of note to hunt, they had to get supplies from The Dalles back east or from Oregon City, their final destination. Barlow wore himself out making long exploratory and relief trips with little nourishment down the steep Zigzag Valley. To make matters miserable, after the wonderfully clear, blue, crisp autumn days, the skies turned dull gray, and they had to deal with a cold rain in the valleys and snow in the passes. Both Barlow and his son William lived through perilous nights when they were stuck soaked and cold to the core, trying to figure out how to get their damp fire starter to work. Then, there were the ice-cold depths of the Sandy River that had to be crossed. Fortunately, the snowfall was relatively light that year, and they were able to avoid disaster.

In the years following, a toll road was built along Barlow's route. It was basically a one-way route that culminated in an outrageously steep slope, misnamed Laurel Hill, where the pioneers had to lower their wagons laboriously and carefully. Besides hacking his way with mere saws and axes to establish a toll road, Barlow resorted to the easier method of setting fires. Before the forests were recognized as a public resource and set aside in preserves, fires burnt vast tracts. Much of what is now the Salmon/Huckleberry Wilderness consists of trees that have grown since the 1900s, with only a few thick, fire-scarred Douglas firs remaining. But the Douglas firs and true firs grow fast in this moist climate of long summer days, as in the case of Bald Mountain, where the view of Mt. Hood has disappeared.

Stretches of the Salmon River and Eagle Creek have a definite rainforest aura to them: the spring ground cover of wood sorrel, the sodden wood debris nursing seedlings, the vine maple limbs clad with lush moss, the long sword ferns, the late-succession-type forest favoring cedars and hemlocks. Over the rolling hills built by volcanism and sunken by glaciers and runoff, Douglas firs thrive in the sun exposure, and viney rhododendrons and a tough ground cover of salal grow profusely on the well-drained inclines. Oregon oaks, which are most prominent along the dry eastside Cascade slopes, find a niche on the south-facing, well-drained volcanic soils of the upper Salmon Creek valley, wet though it may be. Another westside microclimate occurs on the flatlands near the Muddy Fork of the Sandy River where lodgepole pines grow as well as any other tree.

Just to the east of Mt. Hood in the upper Hood River Valley, the annual precipitation drops off markedly, and ponderosa pines and Englemann spruce grow on sun-facing slopes. Whereas on the west side of Hood, the skies remain dreary and dark for most of the winter, the east side is brighter and not extraordinarily cold. These days, not everyone feels the need to cross to the west side, now that smooth, paved roads provide considerably easier access than what Samuel Barlow and company once faced.

South Crater of Mt. Hood

Little North Fork of the Santiam

Santiam

ON OCCASION, FROM ACROSS THE LONG STRETCHES OF ROLLING FORESTLAND, the hard outline of the snowy crest of Mt. Jefferson will emerge from the habitual, puffy cloud layer. Like other areas in the Oregon Cascades, a fiery outpouring from within the earth has created the high points in the Santiam Watershed, most notably Mt. Jefferson. Contrary to more active Cascade volcanoes such as Mt. St. Helens, Jefferson has slumbered for some time and might even be extinct. Its last major eruption occurred before the last two Ice Age advances. Though the incline of the Oregon crest is as a rule gradual, ice and pounding runoff have had time to carve the drainages of Whitewater Creek and Pamelia Creek, which are thickly forested and extend to the base of the mountain, more than a mile below the summit.

Like the parched terrain east of the Cascade Crest the Santiam Watershed is composed of volcanic rock, only now it is covered with exuberant growth, especially of trees. At first, the volcanism was concentrated west of the current crest, and built the mountains, now heavily eroded, which are often called the Western Cascades. Then, the upper Santiam, including what is now Mt. Jefferson, was flooded by fluid flows of basalt that built relatively low-lying shield volcanoes. The older flows were considerably more fluid and of a higher volume than the subsequent eruptions that built Jefferson. This trend follows a typical progression in the southern Cascades and climaxes in the building of stratovolcanoes, where the more recent lava has become thicker, with higher silica content.

The rolling hills and the drenching westside precipitation make for ideal tree-growing conditions, especially for Douglas firs. Impressive noble firs, typically found in clusters with their chinked, purplish bark often covered from the base with bright green moss, tend to grow on the shadier north-facing aspects. As in the North Cascades, prolific western hemlocks and to a lesser extent silver firs thrive in the cool moisture of middle elevations. But of all the vigorous growth in this watershed, the rolling hills and climate particularly favor Douglas firs and undergrowth of rhododendrons on just about every aspect. After the long, almost colorless sleep of winter, when the only color that persists is the dark green of the dormant conifers, the exquisite blooms of pink rhododendron make a brilliant sight in the cloud-shrouded forests. There are viney tangles of them, often accompanied by golden chinquipin, another sprawling and low-lying evergreen. Moss carpets, lush and vibrantly green, flourish in the damp spring air along with a delicate ground cover of miniature dogwood, twinflowers, and pipsessewa. All this exuberant growth occurs under the umbrage of the Douglas firs, those massive furrowed columns that grow to great heights.

The summer climate is hotter and drier than the west side of the North Cascades. On the sun-exposed aspects occasionally grow trees of a more southerly kind, trees of distinction such as sugar pines and incense cedars, and trees and undergrowth with tough leathery leaves such as the Pacific madrone, golden chinquipin, kinnikinnik, snowbrush and salal. These sun-influenced slopes contrast with the dripping rainforest found along low-lying drainages such as the South Fork of the Santiam where the thick, lush growth is much like the drenched valleys common to the north.

Erosion of ancient volcanic extrusions has resulted in soils and rock debris that are far from stable. This instability is quite evident in the vicinity of the Middle Santiam Wilderness, in the slumps and eroded banks along the Middle Santiam River. In general, the profuse vegetation, especially in the older established forests, holds the soils and filters heavy precipitation and runoff. The Little North Fork of the Santiam River drainage, including tributaries such as Opal Creek, contains very clear and pure water, especially in comparison to the downriver watercourses. During the violent floods of February 1996, the streambanks of the Little North Fork were no less affected than any other stream downhill from the snowpack. Its banks were scoured of vegetation, and all sizes of trees, splintered and stripped of bark, were flung along its byways. Yet, despite the ravaged banks, this river did not suffer any lingering affects of excess sediment. The water runs as clear and pure as ever, with emerald depths, crystalline and like jewels.

The first explorers to venture up the Little North Fork of the Santiam to the confluence of Battle Axe Creek and Opal Creek and beyond must have been astonished at the beauty of the place. They would not have been able reach such an interior mountain place with only a casual intent. They would have needed persistence in tumbling down slippery ravines, hacking their way through soaked brush, and stepping over woody debris and thick undergrowth in a deep forest. The lure that impelled the initial exploration was the possibility of great mineral wealth. Some time in the 1860s miners followed a geologic trail that revealed mineral intrusions promising gold, which had surfaced due to the glacial erosion of volcanic rock.

The Little North Fork has continued to be a place of charm and enchantment. But what a place of solitude it must have been to the first explorers, especially in springtime: the fresh, unspoiled spring air, the birds ringing the lonesome wilderness with song, the crystalline water flowing over the polished green and white bedrock, viney rhododendron with lavish pink blooms, the vibrant moss carpets and huckleberry bushes, the rocky cliffs above the North Fork decked with an occasional Pacific madrone, the giant Douglas firs growing in cathedral-like groves.

Rhododendrons and old growth, South Santiam

Mt. Jefferson from Minto Mountain

Ponderosa pines and balsamroot, Metolius drainage

Deschutes

WHEN JOHN CHARLES FREMONT ON HIS SECOND WESTERN EXPEDITION arrived at Fort Vancouver in November 1843, his cartographer, Charles Preuss, wrote in his diary: "To hell with this country where it rains for five months. Even though the other seven are like paradise." Fremont considered the rewards of exploring the West Coast but concluded that the rain and darkness afforded no scenic beauty and gladly considered that the Wilkes Expedition had been collecting information on the west side at that time.

Obviously, he must have known that the westerly route was by far the safest, most assured winter route to California, where they could return to the Great Salt Lake by way of the Colorado Plateau, completing a great arc around the unknown Great Basin. But instead, he chose to purchase supplies at Fort Vancouver and continue south along the east side of the Cascades. This plan of travel required a strong sense of purpose and daring, as it involved traversing unknown territory in the middle of winter, crossing mountain ranges under the dire threat of winter storms. Fremont was not unaware of the dangers involved as he set off south from The Dalles on the Columbia, following the Deschutes River (the Riviere aux Chutes or Fall River as it was then known). But, though they were going to be tested in a dangerous (some would say foolhardy) crossing of the Sierras in later months, the crossing of Oregon by following the Deschutes south was almost enchanting. Fremont wrote that the scenery was much more impressive than traveling along the Snake or the Columbia.

The group consisted of diverse mixture of men—French, German, Canadian, Indian, Whites, and Blacks—twenty-five in total. Most of them were young, including several who were under twenty-one years of age. The fact that they were so diverse and young—young enough not to have accumulated harsh prejudices—might partially explain why they so willingly set out on such a hazardous enterprise, and how they stuck together so well in the face of some very trying circumstances for a full year of hard traveling. Also a part of the group was a scout of some renown, Kit Carson, who would accompany Fremont on a number of other dangerous and hard expeditions, acting with violent loyalty and resourcefulness; another member was Charles Preuss, who produced incredibly detailed drawings and maps as well as a journal.

The weather, at first, was clear and icy cold, as the temperature dipped below zero and water froze solid inside of tents. The clear skies allowed splendid views of the snow-plastered peaks, starting with Mt. Hood, then Mt. Jefferson, Three Fingered Jack, Mt. Washington, and the Three Sisters. These peaks, bleached the purest white in the winter sunlight, rise high in north-south alignment above the Cascade crest, high above the densely forested and rolling highlands.

Fremont noted that in their travels they had not seen a river system with so many waterfalls. From approximately 10–17 million years ago, fluid lava eruptions overspread central Oregon, creating deep layers of basalt. Eruptions of more viscous lava created the Western Cascades and then a shift of the eruptions east to the current crest, as well as a gradual uplift of the terrain, created a climatic barrier between the west and east sides. The Deschutes river system developed out of the drainage patterns of the east side of the Cascade barrier as the water cut deeply and unevenly into the layers of basalt as it was diverted north to the Columbia River.

Fremont's party had to negotiate the deep, narrow chasms that had been carved by the outflows of the White, Warm Springs, and Metolius Rivers. The weather turned benign, speeding their passage and allowing the luxury of carrying extra implements (such as a cannon), which they would later have to abandon. The Metolius River is an outstanding example of an eastside drainage system of the volcanic crest. In pine forest, situated in a valley somewhere between Three Fingered Jack and Black Butte, prolific springs among grasses and bushes mark the source. As these springs converge within several hundred feet, this sudden wetland or waterway becomes a full-fledged river. Throughout the year the gush of crystalline water hardly varies in temperature or flow. Lined with ponderosa pines and incense cedars, it starts north before curving in a wide bend eastward and then cutting deeply into the basalt rock and clay sediments. Fremont was not too busily engaged in the problems of crossing this river (descending the steep-walled canyon, finding a suitable ford, righting a mule that had fallen and turned a load of sugar into something like molasses) not to notice the fish traps set by the Indians. He was informed that the Metolius was a salmon stream, far as it is from the mouth of the Columbia and the raging rapids in between.

The magnificent pine forests that Fremont and others found to be common on the east side of the Cascades are no longer so common. During the summertime the east side becomes extremely dry and extremely susceptible to fire as the sun scorches the landscape. In Fremont's day, large ponderosa pines grew in wide park-like spaces with not much else but grasses; in the south, with hardly even grasses on top of the pumice soil. Over the ages, continual fires have cleared out underbrush, singeing and scorching but sparing the large ponderosa pines protected by their thick, plate-like bark. Fremont's group passed through long stretches of these pine forests, in one particular instance arriving at what appears to be Tumalo Creek:

> After passing for several miles over an artemisia [sagebrush] plain, the trail entered a beautiful pine forest, through which we traveled for several hours; and about 4 o'clock descended into the valley of another large branch, on the bottom of which were spaces of open pines, with occasional meadows of good grass, one in which we encamped. The stream is very swift and deep, and about 40 feet wide, and nearly half frozen over. Among the timber here, are larches 140 feet high, and over 3 feet in diameter. We had tonight the rare sight of a lunar rainbow.

After spending the next day entirely in pine forest, they arrived at the Dillon and Benham Falls area, thunderous stretches of whitewater where the river has been diverted by a relatively recent outpouring of lava. In this vicinity they found an old Indian encampment amidst a grove of very large ponderosas, up to seven feet thick just above the base. As they continued along the main stem of the river, they approached Nez Perce Indians, far from their homeland, apparently using a fine band of horses to venture into the Oregon Cascades. They came upon a broad valley, some ten to twelve miles wide, where they crossed the river and began following the Little Deschutes, the most southerly tributary of the river system.

> Today we had good traveling ground; the trail leading sometimes over rather sandy soils in the pine forest, and sometimes over meadow land along the stream. The great beauty of the country in summer constantly suggested itself to our imaginations, and even now we found it beautiful, as we rode along these meadows, from half a mile to two miles wide.

Fremont missed visiting the upper reaches of the Deschutes, an area explored some years later by Judge John Waldo and friends. Starting around 1880, Judge Waldo annually left his legal affairs, political pursuits, and his home in Salem in order to make summer trips to the hinterlands of the Oregon Cascades. He would use these trips as a remedy for nagging health problems and as an opportunity to revel in what were still untouched, wild places. He and his fellows helped name the lakes where they loved to camp: Waldo, Crescent, O'Dell, and Davis. When they first visited these places, they found no signs of human visitation except for an isolated trapper's cabin or two. Ospreys, bald eagles, kingfishers and loons were the common inhabitants, and the waters teemed with trout. During the bright sun-filled days cooled by summer breezes off the lakes, Waldo and friends lived a kind of hunter's and bachelor's paradise, setting up extended camps, making forays into the surrounding hills on the prowl with their rifles on the lookout for a "fat buck."

It was not an experience they learned to take for granted. Waldo could not help but be annoyed by competition from an increasing number of summer visitors and by something far worse: sheepherders who turned loose their flocks to trample the meadows into dust and droppings. In the summer of 1883, he and his friends made a trek north from a camp at Davis Lake through one of the last remaining Eden gardens. Above Davis Lake the river disappears in a field of lava rock, and as is the case in this part of the country, no streams flow overland from the high Cascades. Clear, cold water comes bursting out of an arid land of sandhills and lodgepole pines. Waldo entered a kind of magical world where the springs formed a maze of channels and a meadowland of several miles, a haven for wild creatures. He named the area Crane Prairie after the prominent sandhill cranes.

Waldo and his friends, as well as the Warm Springs Indians who preceded them that summer and whose trail they followed, were constantly on the hunt. Yet, there are times in his journal entries when he could not help but be struck by the wonder of it all, traveling as they were "like a band of adventurers exploring a new world—leaving civilization far behind them." When a young deer unexpectedly approached them well within shooting distance, and stood there with those dark, curious eyes and alert ears, and an almost airborne sense of graceful motion, he did not pick up his rifle.

East side of Three Fingered Jack

The Cascade Crest north from the South Sister

Lava rock, vine maple, and Douglas fir, upper McKenzie

EAST FROM THE THRIVING CENTER OF BEND the land becomes increasingly parched as the oasis of the Cascades, the lush life-provider, becomes increasingly distant. On the last leg of their journey across the continent the pioneers of the last century must have felt keenly this contrast. The Oregon desert extends over a vast flatland with denuded hills and ragged clouds that linger at the edge of a scorching sun-filled sky. Clouds appear like an illusion, for they hardly ever seem to be overhead, but in the distance on an unattainable horizon. At first the western juniper trees are plentiful, thriving where the pines have long since given up. But they dwindle and then disappear amidst the sage, the scrawny desiccated grass, and baked volcanic rocks.

In 1853, Elijah Elliot, who had previously made the journey to the Willamette Valley, traveled east to meet his family at Boise. He agreed to lead a loose contingent of wagons on a more direct route to the Cascades, across the Oregon desert to a newly built road that traversed the mountains at Willamette Pass, next to the landmark of Diamond Peak.

Once his group parted with the Malheur River, good water became increasingly difficult to find; and worse, the group became disoriented and wasted valuable time going the wrong way. On September 10, Elliot dispatched two groups to scout ahead to alert people on the west side that they were waylaid and suffering for provisions. Unfortunately, the scouts missed the blazes of the faint trail south that would have taken them across Willamette Pass, the proposed route. Instead, they headed due west toward the Three Sisters, and at least one group wandered across the crest just north of the South Sister, around Chambers Lake. At a high point they were able to view what they thought was Diamond Peak to the south, but they chose to continue directly west into the South Fork of the McKenzie.

The natives at that time used trails across the crest to make an annual trek to the McKenzie Valley. Apparently, they preferred the cold and relatively clear winters of the east side to the interminable rain and clouds of the west. In the spring and summer they sought the wealth of salmon and trout in the McKenzie, and on their way back in the fall they picked and preserved huckleberries. They also made frequent trips to the west side of the Middle Sister, to the obsidian cliffs, the fields and ravines of glass, in order to obtain material for sharp objects. However, the mountains were not a place where the natives ever felt at home, and they left barely a mark. In their disorientation the scouts would sometimes follow what they thought were Indian trails, but few of these led to where they thought they wanted to go.

By the time the scouts had crossed the crest, they had run out of provisions. If they had been better hunters, they probably would not have suffered as much as they did for food. It being the autumn season, the hills were full of ripe huckleberries; the McKenzie River was full of fish; and though much of the area was wooded, there must have been sufficient deer as well as easily hunted grouse. As the two groups passed each other, there was some indication of rivalry between them. The group that had a dog was faring better because the dog had helped them corner a deer and a bear. Faithful as the dog was, he would end up as a meal, as dogs often did in those days, whether to Lewis and Clark or the natives. In any event, it is unfortunate that these pioneers were so poor that they could not better appreciate the wonders and mystery of the place, since they were visiting uncharted territory. In their half-starved condition, they could see no beauty in the forests, having to spend most of their efforts clawing through the dense thickets or struggling up steep, slippery slopes bounding the river. The mountain places had become their enemy, and they were most eager to be rescued and escorted to their destination, the Willamette Valley, where they would go on to establish farmlands and settlements.

The McKenzie River, as well as the Santiam, is a major tributary of the Willamette, the main river system that trends north to the Columbia and creates a vast tract of fertile farmland. The central Oregon Cascades, a center of volcanism both old and new, creates a highland divide of snow-capped peaks, a source of these river systems. The centerpiece is the three stratovolcanos called the Three Sisters whose snowy summits rise more than 10,000 feet and are aligned in close proximity along the crest. But these mountains are only the beginning of the volcanism. More than one hundred eruptions have occurred between the North Sister and Three Fingered Jack since the last Ice Age, in the last 10,000 years. Much of the McKenzie Pass area continues to appear as a wasteland of dark lava rock, bare except for lichens, interspersed with bleached snags of whitebark pines or subalpine firs.

Some of the relatively recent lava flows have run into the North Fork of the McKenzie, causing a unique drainage system consisting of intermittent and underground watercourses. The most recent basalt flow from the Belknap crater blocked the North Fork, creating the aptly named Clear Lake with its ghostly, underwater forest. Part of the main channel now runs dry in the summer, and in one section the river emerges from its underground course in a beautiful turquoise pool, Tamolith Pool. Ancient, venerable forests of mostly large Douglas firs grow along Hackleman Creek and near Clear Lake toward the upper north part of the watershed. This upper watershed is a unique place of plant diversity. Ancient Alaska yellow cedars, typically found in the wet, colder climes north grow unusually large in Echo Basin, while on nearby sunny slopes grow incense cedars, more fond of the heat and sun of the south. Douglas firs and, increasingly, incense cedars farther south combine with the autumn-brilliant vine maples amongst the dark, abrasive rocks in the valley.

Paintbrush and larkspur, Cone Peak

Alaska yellow cedar, Echo Basin

Upper Proxy Falls

Rhododendrum, ferns, incense cedars, North Umpqua

Umpqua

In 1824, David Douglas was sent on a mission by the Royal Horticultural Society of London and the Hudson's Bay Company to collect unknown plant specimens along the Pacific Coast, and in the autumn of 1826, he subsequently joined an organized effort to explore southern Oregon. At this time, not a great deal was known about the interior of the Cascade Range. It was still not known, for example, whether there was a southern waterway such as the Columbia that would link the Rocky Mountains with the West Coast. The purpose of this expedition was to extend the control of territory for the British fur traders whose base was Fort Vancouver along the Columbia River. Indians still had free reign over the western river valleys. It was before the time when smallpox and other European diseases began to wipe out their ranks and before settlers started laying claims to tribal land. Bands of Indians as well as grizzly bears roamed the land free and unimpeded, and neither took too kindly to efforts to restrict their freedom.

Douglas had spent the earlier months of the year exploring the interior of the Columbia, the lower stretches of the Snake, and the Blue Mountains, constantly on the move from March through September with the unbending purpose of exploring the life and topography of the land; bringing back specimens and tokens; suffering through hunger, deluges of water, dehydration, lack of sleep, extremes of temperature, and isolation in the company of natives who did not share the same language or intentions. The natives called him the Man of Grass. He amazed them when he wore his spectacles, started fires by using a glass, or drank boiled water.

Douglas's main intention in embarking on this dangerous adventure was to find and collect specimens of giant pine trees growing somewhere along the headwaters of the Willamette River. He had heard stories about their enormous size and seen the pinecones, more than a foot long and like nothing he had ever seen before, and was eager to explore to the source of this mystery. Though Douglas and his companions started with fine weather during September, it was not long before the rainy season descended with short, dark days and soaking, bone-chilling rain. They brought hardly any nonperishable food, and much of their attention on the trip was taken by hunting deer, elk, waterfowl, squirrels—just about anything they could shoot. Acting on tips and the help of Indian guides, Douglas separated from his companions and headed east following the Umpqua River over steep hills in search of the pine. He had to depend on the Indians not only for direction, but also for food, often in the form of dried salmon; and they offered him hospitality and kindness, especially when he was injured and in need. As in Douglas's other trips, he would push himself to exhaustion, exposed to the raw elements, often to an injured state, without knowing where he could find his next nourishment.

As he drew closer to the object of his hard journey, he was hit by a ferocious storm that blew down his tent, toppled trees, and left him soaked and sleepless. As the wind roared and the rain fell in sheets, he huddled against the frightened horses. He relates how in the morning he rubbed his benumbed body with a handkerchief before the fire until he could no longer endure the pain. Feeling ill from a headache, impaired vision, and an upset stomach, he had to make do without any available medicine. The only available remedy was to force himself into a sweat, and that worked only slightly. That night he came upon Indian lodges where natives gave him salmon that was hardly edible; otherwise, he would have gone hungry that entire day. It must have been an ominous, unnerving experience for one who was accustomed to enduring all sorts of privations in order to discover plants.

The next day he succeeded in locating a magnificent untouched grove and collecting specimens, but not without incident. Indicative of the fact that the local Indians probably collected the large cones for the seeds, he was not able to find any on the ground. The fierce storm had no doubt blown down a plethora of them, which must have all been collected by local food gatherers. He started firing his gun at the cones high in the trees. The sudden gunfire attracted the attention of armed, war-painted Indians who were suspicious about his intentions. In his previous explorations up the Columbia, he had shown a talent for diplomacy with hostile natives, and some luck in avoiding encounters, perhaps much of it due to the fact that they never knew what to make of him. The other white men tended to act as if they had something to gain at their expense, but this man was somehow content with gathering plants, pushing himself and his guides in unaccountable ways. Douglas had to put his skills to use to evade these natives, and he spent the next several nights anxiously worrying about their sudden reappearance.

He described his discovery in his journal:

"New or strange things seldom fail to make great impressions, and often we are liable to over-rate them; and lest I should never see my friends to tell them verbally of this most beautiful and immensely large tree, I now state the dimensions of the largest one I could find that was blown down by the wind: Three feet from the ground, 57 feet 9 inches in circumference; 134 feet from the ground, 17 feet 5 inches; extreme length 215 feet."

Some have disputed the "57 feet 9 inches in circumference," especially since he also described these trees as "remarkably straight," and also because no one since has found a sugar pine approaching the same girth.

On the way out, rather than being visited by hostile Indians, he ran into a grizzly sow and her two cubs. They had scared the daylights out of his guide the preceding night. He relates how he calmly and deliberately approached within twenty yards while they were feeding on acorns in a clearing, and then gunned them down when they defiantly arose and growled. In his journals he offers a meditation at one infrequent moment of rest when he was observing young trout swimming in a pool of water. He soon realized that the placid scene contained a deadly game: the larger fish were trying to outwit and consume the smaller fish. The scene reflected the warlike conditions of the frontier, where it was the accepted behavior of the explorers to venture into the unknown with violence.

During the three weeks it took to return to the outpost of Fort Vancouver, Douglas experienced firsthand the weather in the Pacific Northwest during November. Day after day the "rain fell in torrents" as his party struggled not just to stay dry because that was impossible, but merely to keep going, to bypass the flooding river channels, and find enough nourishment off the all-encompassing, dreary, soaked land. After a day battling to ford the swollen streams in a cold, driving rain without anything to eat, there were occasions when they had to bed down, exhausted, in wet blankets. He took heart from the spirit of the voyageurs:

"There is a curious feeling among voyageurs. One who complains of hunger or indeed of hardship of any description, things that in any other country would be termed extreme misery, is hooted and brow-beaten by the whole party as a pork-eater or a young voyageur, as they term it."

Today, the huge sugar pines, which Douglas and others subsequently reported, are long gone. The grizzly bears are also gone, and the nomadic Indians no longer have free use of the land. The salmon and steelhead also have become mostly relics of the past. Yet, one can still wander along the swirling and dashing emerald waters of the North Umpqua, below the singular basalt rock formations of Rattlesnake Rock and Eagle Rock; and perhaps on a drizzly fall day when the vine maples leaves are a watercolored scarlet, still come upon the battered remains of a giant salmon that has somehow managed to make an unlikely return.

The vegetation of this area is considerably different from the North Cascades, as plants that typically do well in more southerly climes become prolific along the westside slopes. Actually, there is a convergence of trees from all directions that flourish in this watershed. Beautiful and distinctive trees, notably sugar pines and incense cedars, find their way north from the mountains of California, and in some places find their fullest expression. The Pacific madrone, a remarkable tree of leathery green leaves and bare, barkless limbs, spreads into the mountains from the coast and, on some lower elevation hills, almost forms entire forests. Eastside trees, notably ponderosa pines, have migrated west of the crest and grow to large proportions on south-facing slopes. Then, the common Oregon westside association of Douglas firs, western hemlocks, and rhododendrons extends from the north and flourishes on the shadier, wetter slopes.

If the sugar pines are no longer so evident, the incense cedars of the Rogue-Umpqua divide are still a wonder. They grow on the lower elevation south sides, along with Pacific madrones and ponderosa pines, scorched by the sun and frequent fires. But they also grow at higher elevations, especially prominent in open, grassy meadows frequented by elk. They make a very singular appearance: ennobled by age, gothic, with ghostly, sprawling limbs and thick, ribbed bark ranging in shade from an ashen gray to a deep mahogany, depending on the sun exposure.

The ridges and high points of places such as the Boulder Creek drainage as well as the upper reaches of the South Umpqua River represent older volcanic activity that has since shifted to the east, roughly to the current Cascade crest. The headwaters of the North Umpqua River arise in the vicinity of the Cascade crest, terrain of a quite different character than the westside hills. Long stretches of lodgepole pines grow on a Yellowstone-like plateau of porous, sandy pumice soils. Occasionally, an eroded cone or knob interrupts the flat surface, and lakes such as Lemelo and Diamond interrupt the green. The notable anomaly of this rather monotonous landscape is the pointy spire of the high point of the watershed: Mt. Thielsen. Thielsen is similar to other remnant volcanoes such as Mt. Washington and Three Fingered Jack in that the outer shield has been eroded away, exposing the harder volcanic plug. The slightly tilted spire, more like a needle, has come to be known as "the lightning rod of the Cascades," as its obviously exposed position attracts bolts of lightning from the storms that are common here in the summer.

During the summer season the sun burns through the long days, baking the landscape in the dry air. The dust becomes thick on the trail, and there is the resiny pine fragrance, the brown needles spread over the parched ground, the desiccated and brittle snags waiting for fire and horrific winds to renew another lodgepole pine cycle. Higher up, mountain hemlocks predominate, growing shaggy, thick and old, mingling with scattered clumps of upright, scaly whitebark pines. The sheer north side of Mt. Thielsen, consisting of twisted red and dark rock, hewn over the ages by glacial action, rises above a long apron of rubble extending down to the outlet creek. Not much is left of the glacier, lying shrunken and broken at the base of the north wall. But the action of the deep snows of the winter is still awesome, judging by the mountain hemlocks recently split and bent by avalanches at the base of the lower rock field.

Incense cedars at Lonesome Meadows

Pacific madrona, North Umpqua

North side of Mt. Thielsen

Autumn along the Rogue River

ABOVE THE RUSHING WATERS OF THE UPPER ROGUE RIVER, there is nothing very dramatic rising above the landscape. South of Mt. Thielsen for a good distance, a few rock outcrops stick above the crest but not much more until Mt. McLoughlin. It is not very surprising that the first non-Indian explorer, a fortune-seeker straying far off course from the trail of gold, almost fell into Crater Lake before noticing it. Not that Crater Lake does not catch the eye, but it is set high on the crest, cradled by eroded and ruined ridges of an old volcano, and the rim, which is often forested with large mountain hemlocks and Shasta red firs, appears without much warning.

The natives viewed Crater Lake as a place of power and mystery and were in awe of its natural presence, the incredible expanse of blue. They did not readily escort European explorers to its hidden location, but considered it sacred and the knowledge of its presence a secret. Those who sought the Spirit for insight or power ventured there on vision quests, fasting for long periods of time, descending the steep talus slopes to the lake.

The ruined volcano, which once rose in place of the present Crater Lake, has been called Mt. Mazama. One day some 7,000 years ago, it exploded with an incredible violence, unimaginable even in comparison with the 1980 St. Helens eruption. When it was over, about a mile-high mountain had been blown into the air, collapsing the caldera into an enormous crater, thousands of feet deep, raining down ash and pumice onto the landscape to the northeast. Areas near Crater Lake received as much as twenty feet of pumice and a layer six inches thick was spread as far as one hundred miles north along the Cascade crest.

After the long prelude leading to the final eruption, it is hard to imagine that any Native Americans, who had long since migrated down the West Coast, were anywhere near the place. Considering the rumblings and explosions from forces that were beyond any ordinary description or explanation, they had probably fled for their lives. Then, after the final eruption had destroyed everything within a radius of about thirty-five miles, no one would have ventured anywhere close to the crater for a very long time. The fallout, the ash and dust that could have created an awful and longstanding miasma, would have been reason alone, not to mention the loss of vital food supplies.

Probably only after the place had assumed a tranquil presence, after the water had filled the blasted-out crater, did the most venturesome and brave dare to journey to the rim. They were confronting forces far beyond anything that they could afford to consider ordinary. Looking out on all that mesmerizing beauty, they saw the work of spirits that created and changed the landscape, impossible to predict or to know. They felt great fear and wondered if these same entities that had sprung such violence would also throw their fragile bodies into the dark waters. They found that when they were daring enough to suffer privations and to enter these mysterious realms, they were given visionary powers.

From the lonely high points around the lake, such as from Mt. Scott, John Waldo was able to get a wide-open view extending to Lake Klamath and Mt. Shasta to the south. The crest becomes far more gradual southward, much easier to travel, and there are wide-open flats to the east. Waldo spent some time watching antelopes, noting their nervous habits, how they were ever on the alert for the slightest disturbance that would send them running with the "speed of the wind with a long train of dust behind them." As was often the case in his journal entries, he was torn between the desire to hunt and a reverence for the innocence and beauty of wild creatures.

In the summer of 1888, Waldo and his companions traveled the lower stretch of the Cascade Crest from Crater Lake to Mt. Shasta. Although at that time a wagon road provided access between Lake Klamath and the Ashland area, much of the crest above the upper Rogue was still remote and seldom visited. Waldo reported that they had easy traveling through meadows and strongly scented mountain forest until they came to a deeply cut ravine, an upper drainage of the Rogue River. He wrote that "a wilder spot or more inaccessible I have not seen in the mountains." Going farther south, his group climbed the solitary volcanic cone of Mt. McLoughlin and reached other high points. South of the Klamath River, he described the stretch leading to Mt. Shasta as one big "sheep corral."

Though the Rogue River Valley drains the west side of the Cascades, the climate becomes progressively drier and the rhododendrons disappear. The summers, in particular, are hotter and drier than the lusher northerly forests. Douglas firs, their deep-furrowed bark rough and pocked with holes, have grown ancient in the dry air. The pine forests, with open spaces covered with pine straw and grasses, feature two of nature's greatest pine trees, the ponderosa pine and sugar pine, as well as western white pine, which also can grow to large sizes. Only scant remnants can be found now of the magnificent forest that once grew to great proportions on the rich volcanic soil left by the old Mt. Mazama.

Crater Lake

Rogue River and lava rock near Natural Bridge

References:

Allen, John Eliot. *The Magnificent Gateway:*
A Layman's Guide to the Geology of the Columbia River Gorge.
Portland, OR: Timber Press, 1979.

Beckey, Fred. *Range of Glaciers.*
Portland, OR: Oregon Historical Society Press, 2003.

Brogan, Phil F. *East of the Cascades,*
Portland, OR: Binfords and Mort, 1964.

Bruseth, Nels. *Indian Stories and Legends*
of the Stillaquamish, Sauks And Allied Tribes.
Fairfield, WA: Ye Galleon Press, 1977.

Coleman, Edmund T. *First Ascent of Mt. Baker;*
Mountaineering on the Pacific.
Seattle: Shorey, 1966.

Connolly, Dolly.
Sports Illustrated. "Mighty Joe Morovits." January 7, 1963.

Del Grosso, Robert C. *Rail Fan's Guide to Stampede and Stevens Passes.*
Great Northern Pacific Publications, 1997.

Douglas, David. *The Oregon Journals of David Douglas.*
Ashland, OR: Oregon Book Society, 1972.

Douglas, William O. *Of Men and Mountains.*
New York: Harper, 1950.

Fremont, John Charles.
The Exploring Expedition to the Rocky Mountains, Oregon and California.
Buffalo, NY: Auburn, Derby and Miller, 1854.

Grauer, Jack. *Mt. Hood: A Complete History.*
Grauer, 1975.
An account of Samual Barlow's Mt. Hood experiences.

Guggenheim, Alan. *Spirit Lake People.*
Gresham, OR: Salem, Press 1986.

Harmon, Rick. *Crater Lake National Park: A History.*
Corvallis, OR: Oregon State University Press, 2002.

Harris, Stephen L. *Fire Mountains of the West:*
The Cascade and Mono Lake Volcanoes.
Missoula, MT: Mountain Press, 1988.
Main reference for the history of volcanism in the Northwest.

Hult, Ruby El. *Northwest Disaster: Avalanche and Fire.*
Portland, OR: Binfords & Mort, 1960.
An account of the Wellington disaster.

Jenkins, Will D. *Last Frontier in the North Cascades:*
Tales of the Wild Upper Skagit.
Mt. Vernon, WA: Skagit County Historical Society, 1984.

Majors, Harry M. and Richard C. McCollum, editors.
Northwest Discovery, The Journal of Northwest History and Natural History.
 v.1-6 (June 1980-1988).
Contains reports by Henry Custer, Henry Pierce, D. C. Linsley,
Hazard Stevens, August V. Kautz, Edward S. Ingraham, John C. Fremont.

Majors, Harry M., editor.
Mt. Baker: A Chronicle of its Historic Eruptions and First Ascent.
Seattle: Northwest Press, 1978.

McClure, Andrew S. *The Diary of Andrew S. McClure.*
Oregon: Lane County Historical Society, 1959.
Account of the Elijah Elliot Journey in 1853.

McNeil, Fred H. *Mt. Hood: Wy'east, the Mountain Revisited.*
Zigzag, OR: Zig Zag Papers, 1990.

Moulton, Gary E., ed. *The Definitive Journals of Lewis and Clark.*
Down the Columbia to Fort Clatsop.
Lincoln: University of Nebraska, 1990.

Muir, John. *Steep Trails.* Edited by William Frederic Bade.
Boston: Houghton Mifflin, 1918.

Norman, Elof. *The Coffee Chased Us Up: Monte Cristo Memories.*
Seattle: Mountaineers, 1977.

Owen, Benjamin Franklin. *My Trip across the Plains.*
Oregon: Lane County Historical Society, 1959.
Account of the Elijah Elliot Journey in 1853.

Prater, Yvonne. *Snoqualmie Pass: From Indian Trail to Interstate.*
Seattle: Mountaineers, 1981.

Ross, Alexander. *The Fur Hunters of the Far West.*
Edited by Kenneth A. Spalding, Norman: University of Oklahoma, 1956.

Tabor, Rowland and Ralph Haugerud.
Geology of the North Cascades: A Mountain Mosaic.
Seattle: Mountaineers, 1999.

Waldo, John. *Letters and Journals of the High Cascades.*
Available online: www.fs.jorge.com/archives/Waldo.

Williams, Chuck. *Bridge of the Gods, Mountains of Fire:*
A Return to the Columbia Gorge.
New York : Friends of the Earth, 1980.

Willis, Margaret. *Checkacos All, The Pioneering of the Skagit.*
Mt. Vernon, WA: Skagit County Historical Society, 1973.

Winthrop Associates Cultural Research.
The Klamath Indians of Southern Oregon Cascades.
Available online: www.nps.gov/crla/klsoc.htm.

Winthrop, Theodore. *Canoe and Saddle.*
Portland, OR: Binfords and Mort, 1955.

Woodhouse, Phillip R. *Monte Cristo.*
Seattle: Mountaineers, 1979.